# Hoodoo Medicine

## Gullah Herbal Remedies

*Miss Myma, a Sea Islands resident wise in plant lore, 1974.*

*In roadside patches like this one, many healing plants can be found.*

# Hoodoo Medicine

## Gullah Herbal Remedies

Text and Photographs by Faith Mitchell

Illustrations by Naomi Steinfeld

Originally published in Columbia, South Carolina
by Summerhouse Press



Library of Congress Cataloging Information

Mitchell, Faith
Hoodoo medicine: Gullah herbal remedies / by Faith Mitchell. --
Rev. ed.
p. cm.
Includes bibliographical references and index.
ISBN 1-887714-33-2
1. Gullahs--Folklore. 2. Gullahs--Medicine. 3. Gullahs-
-Ethnobotany. 4. Traditional medicine--Sea Islands. 5 Medicinal
plants--Sea Islands. 6. Ethnobotany--Sea Islands. I. Title.
GR111.A47M57 1998
398'.353--dc21 98-29389
CIP

Cover art: "Quiet Time" 1994
Acrylic on canvas, 16"x20"
by Jonathan Green

# *Contents*

# *The Island Speaks*

my lushness:
resting in my arms
cradled in my love of life
are the swamps and
grasses,
the million flights
and songs,
cries in verdant jubilation,
the silverings in the sun
of my salt creeks,
my muddy flows of tears;
the snails curved pink,
chalky oysters,
angry timid crabs.

Amid the splashings
and cries
and singing,
under the tropic
umbrella
of the web of light,
nestled in my
mossy loving fingers,
are my people;
the slow-moving,
warm and loving families—
offspring of tears
and desolation darker and
denser than ever my own;
semi-sweet;
children of afternoons
that were close and dark ceilinged in

*The silverings in the sun of salt creeks.*

low gray doom
and lit with charges
of angry electricity;
a handful of simplicity:
shy, neglected, surviving;
caught in my shimmering embrace
like thick drops thrown up
against the sky;
caught in my blues
and greens,
my salty musty gentle kisses:
my people.
Cupped in my hand,
in their trying
and bursting forth:
my own.

*Boats at low tide on Wadmalaw Island, 1974.*

*An old cauldron that was still being used.*

# *Preface*

The Sea Islands, although rapidly changing, remain a unique and beautiful center of Afro-American culture. With the renewed contemporary interest in rural life and the world of nature, it seemed time for a book contributing the knowledge of black Americans, a people who have always lived closely and peacefully with the earth.

I have received invaluable assistance in my research and writing from many people. Among them I wish to thank Dr. Niara Sudarkasa, Bamidele Agbasegbe, Patricia J. Jackson, and my friends and acquaintances from the Sea Islands. Many thanks to Ishmael Reed for his permission to reprint this book. I dedicate it to Archie and Alexis.

—Faith Mitchell
1998

*Fennel, conveniently growing in a yard.*

# Introduction

The first section of this book traces the history of the Sea Islands, and describes the black traditional medical system of which herbal medicine is one component. The warm, temperate climate of South Carolina and other southern states supports few of the wild plants that grow in West Africa. Some cultivated African crops, such as okra and peanuts, grow in the southern United States, but the wild plants are largely dissimilar. Without access to wild plants similar to those of their homeland, the enslaved Africans had to adapt their herbal medical knowledge to the new environment. We know that this adaptation was made. How it was made is not so obvious. The third and fourth chapters explore this problem.

In the second section, the medicinal plants used in the Sea Islands are described and discussed. The information in this section is the result of my own research in the South Carolina Sea Islands in 1974. To my own research material I have added contrasting southern black, native American, and Euro-American usages of the same plants. The Euro-American uses are drawn primarily from books written in the nineteenth and early twentieth centuries—periods when herbal medicine was well documented and widely used. The southern black references are both historical and contemporary; native American references are historical.

*An old wooden cottage, with shutters in the place of glass, Wadmalaw Island, 1974.*

*The tools of a low-country farmer.*

# Chapter 1

## A Brief History of the Sea Islands

The island chain called the Sea Islands extends from the coast of North Carolina, along South Carolina and Georgia, to the northern edge of Florida, bordering the Atlantic Ocean. The islands are lush and low lying; they are separated from each other and the mainland by hundreds of creeks, marshes, and rivers. As will be described in this chapter, three factors were primarily responsible for the unique position of the Sea Islands in black American history. First was the predominance of blacks in the population. South Carolina led the other slave states in the percentage of slaves in the population and, within the state, the largest number of slaves resided in the Sea Islands.

Second was the isolation of the islands, which until the 1930s were accessible only by boat. On smaller plantations, slaves probably encountered only a handful of whites — the owner and his family — while on the larger ones months might pass with only one white, the overseer, in residence. On some plantations even the drivers and overseers were black.

> The overseer...is the only white man upon the place, besides the owner, who is always absent during the sickly months of the summer. All the engineers, millers, smiths, carpenters and sailers, are black.[1]

The third important factor was the ongoing importation into South Carolina of slaves brought directly from Africa. Legislation passed in the early part of the eighteenth century placed lower duties on slaves imported directly from Africa than on those brought to South Carolina from other states or elsewhere in the New World. In addition, the isolation of the islands made it possible for slaves to be landed there long after passage of the Slave Trade Act of 1808, which was supposed to end the African slave trade.

The end result of these circumstances was the persistence of African culture in the Sea Islands for a longer time and more strongly than in any other part of the United States.

## African Origins

The southeastern United States was originally the home of dozens of Indian nations that were culturally part of the Mississippian civilization. The descendants of these tribes would later be known as Choctaws, Chickasaws, Cherokees, Creeks, and Natchez.[2] The first Africans came to these Indian lands in 1526, as members of a Spanish expedition that was exploring the coast north of Florida. It would be another 150 years before Europeans and Africans settled permanently on what is now the South Carolina coast. In the meantime, for the remainder of the 16th century, French and Spanish settlers fought fruitlessly to establish coastal dominance, battling each other and the local Indians. Blacks served both the French and Spanish sides, and some eventually went to live with Indian groups.[3] In the 1660s the English entered the scene, but they were not successful in establishing themselves until 1670, when English planters from Barbados made a permanent settlement in Carolina on the west bank of a river they named the Ashley. With that, blacks became permanent residents of the coast.

The first black settlers known to us by name were "John Sr., Elizabeth, and John Jr.," a slave family from Bermuda who arrived in the colony in September, 1670.[4] They were the first of a trickle of slaves that rapidly became a flood of black settlement as evidence of the fertile potential of the coastal lands increased the demand for slave labor. By 1710, blacks slightly outnumbered whites in the Carolina colony, with 4,100 slaves to 4,080 whites.[5] By the 1790 census, slaves were 72% of the population in the coastal counties of Georgetown, Charleston and Beaufort, where there was a total population of 78,000 slaves to 29,860 whites.[6]

In 1860, as the South entered the Civil War, the Sea Islands were still predominantly black, with a population that was 73% slave and 27% white.[7] After the Civil War, and the collapse of the plantation economy, the white population diminished, then decades later climbed on some islands (e.g., James Island and Hilton Head) as a result of post-World War II suburbanization. Meanwhile, the black population shrank as people left to find work elsewhere. At the time of my research, in the late 1970's, about 37% of the population was black on five major South Carolina Sea Islands.[8]

A lot remains to be learned about the countries and tribal groups that were home to the African slaves brought to the Sea Islands. However, records of the day, such as ships' logs and newspaper notices, provide tantalizing hints. A list compiled by Littlefield[9] of slaves of African origin living in colonial South Carolina included these groups: Kisi, Bossue, Coromantee, Cromttey, Gambia, Malagoacow, Guinea, Mandingo, Ibo, and Angola. In terms of present-day countries, this list represents a large section of the Atlantic coast of West Africa, beginning around what is now Liberia and continuing south to the country of Angola.

Another list, this time of slave imports into Charleston between 1735 and 1740, indicated that most of the slaves were from Angola, with a small number coming from the Gambia, the Windward and Gold Coast (the area west of, and including, present-day Ghana), and Bonny in what is now Nigeria.[10]

Newspaper notices for runaway slaves give additional detail about their origins and also suggest the individual personalities of these Africans. For example, one advertisement was for "two tall likely young new Bambara negro fellows..." referring to the Bambara tribe of Mali. Another was for "a short chubby hairy Angola fellow..."[11] Some descriptions refer to tribal markings borne by the Africans, such as lines along their noses and foreheads or on their upper bodies, or to the fact that some of the slaves' teeth had been shaped or filed to make them more attractive by African standards.[12]

Another source of information about the African origins of the Gullah people is the Gullah dialect itself. Lorenzo Turner's groundbreaking research in the thirties found words in the Gullah vocabulary from the following languages of the African Atlantic coast: Wolof, Malinke, Mandinka, Bambara, Fula, Mende, Vai, Twi, Fante, Ga, Ewe, Fon, Yoruba, Bini, Hausa, Ibo, Ibibio, Efik, Kongo, Umbundu, and Kimbundu.[13]

## The Plantations

Contrary to popular image, the first settlers of South Carolina did not raise cash crops, but livestock. Taking advantage of the abundance of land, the English developed large herds which they milked, slaughtered for local consumption or shipment to Barbados, and sold to new settlers. Slaves were often responsible for caring for the livestock, which involved such activities as fencing lands for pasture, building pens for calves, and hunting down strays. Some of the Africans brought to South Carolina in that period may have had prior experience tending herds, if they came from those parts of west Africa where livestock were kept.[14]

With time, raising livestock gave way to the enormous rice plantations for which Carolina became famous. One planter owned 2,087 slaves spread over fourteen rice plantations; another had 700 slaves on one plantation. By the mid-18th century, rice was to the South Carolina economy what tobacco was to Maryland and Virginia. Today, the old rice fields have reverted to marshland, but paddies once lined the coast. The slaves were central to maintaining them, and there is good evidence that their prior experience with rice growing provided the critical edge that allowed the English settlers to become so successful in this new arena.

Rice culture involves specific techniques for planting, growing, and harvesting the grain, with carefully timed cycles of flooding and drying the fields. The English who settled Carolina knew none of these techniques in the late 1690s when they made their first tentative efforts at cultivation. However, blacks from the west coast of Africa, where rice is widely cultivated, were familiar with the necessary processes. References can be found in notices of slave sales, and even in the records of the *Amistad* trial, to African knowledge of rice cultivation.[15] In Carolina, the slaves handled rice in traditional African ways, singing in unison as they moved through the fields in rows, winnowing the grain with wide, flat handwoven baskets, and separating the grain from the husks with wooden mortars and pestles.[16]

In the 1740s, indigo, prized for the natural blue colors obtained from its leaflets and branches, was introduced to Carolina plantations, followed in the 1790s by the premium cotton known as Sea-Island cotton. Sea-Island cotton grew very well in the sandy soil found along the South Carolina coast and within a short time it was cultivated widely. The trio of rice, indigo, and cotton was the backbone of the coastal plantation economy from the end of the 18th century until the Civil War.

After the Civil War, the economic livelihood of the coast progressed, in stages, from turpentine production, with its detrimental effects on the forests, to attempts to rejuvenate rice planting, to lumbering, which again reduced forestland. In the twentieth century, the economy shifted to agricultural crops, such as tomatoes, and commercial fishing. As it became increasingly difficult for the local economy to support families, an outmigration of young people began. Already, by the twenties, many black communities were characterized by a predominance of older people, in whose hands was left the care of grandchildren and grandnieces and nephews, while the working-age generation was living elsewhere, in Charleston, North Carolina, or father afield. In the 1930s, the first bridges connecting the Sea Islands and the mainland were built. Even then, the long distances involved made frequent travel prohibitive and the islands remained isolated. There are some islands that can still be reached only by boat.

Until recently, black Sea Island communities were ignored and neglected by local authorities. Beyond rudimentary attention by government to roads and segregated schools, the Islanders were left to their own devices, good or bad. For example, in the twenties, black schools on St. Helena island had an average of 75 students per teacher and received only enough money from the state for five months of instruction. There were no black voters on the island and only 20 whites who were qualified to vote.[17] In the seventies, at the time of my research, the standard of living on the islands was still very low and many houses lacked electricity, telephones, and plumbing. There was no public transporation and services like health care were extremely limited. To the extent that external attention was directed to the islands, too often it was for the purpose of uprooting families from scenic properties that had become attractive to outsiders.

Today, there is renewed interest in Gullah culture and an understanding of its unique contributions and importance. It could not come at a more critical time, for this culture is in danger of declining as the older generation dies and the younger people, whose horizons are broader than their elders ever dreamed, are more attracted by the wider world than by the folk culture of yesteryear.

## Plantation Life and Gullah Culture

On the plantations, life for the slaves was governed by the cycle of the planting season. Rice, for example, was worked almost entirely by hand, beginning with the preparation of the fields in March, seed planting in April, hoeing during the summer, harvesting in September, and threshing, winnowing, and pounding to remove the husk in the fall. In the period after the first flooding of the fields, when the rice did not need immediate attention, the slaves' efforts shifted to higher ground, where they planted potatoes, corn, collards, peas, and other crops for plantation consumption.[18]

While cultivation was the main activity on the plantation, the slaves had many other jobs as well. There was wood work of various kinds, including chopping and sawing timber, splitting fence rails, slicing shingles, and shaping and pitching barrels. There was also blacksmithing and iron working. Fish teemed in the streams of the low country, and some slaves knew how to poison them, using a mixture of quicklime and plant extracts that was added to the water. The practice was technically a misdemeanor, but it continued nonetheless.[19] Drawing on the West African familiarity with crocodiles, there were also slaves who knew how to handle these creatures, which terrified the whites. The slaves also mastered the manufacture of dugout canoes from cypress logs. Before roads and bridges were well established, these boats were the primary means of navigating the coastal marshes.

Another long list of jobs was associated with the plantation household. These included cooks, housekeepers, minders of both slave and white babies, maids, butchers, weavers, laundresses, and seamstresses. Many of the skilled slaves would have been trained in more than one of these occupations.[20]

In the time remaining after a full day of work and during the free time they were allowed on weekends, slave families tried as they could to attend to their own needs. In addition to cooking, childrearing, gardening, and fishing, these hours were the time for spiritual worship at a secluded praise house, for storytelling, singing, dancing, and other activities, like woodcarving and mat weaving, that were part of the Gullah culture.

The hallmark of Sea Island folk culture was its oral heritage of stories and songs, and its distinctive Gullah dialect, formerly called Geechee. Before Lorenzo Turner's definitive research, some writers ascribed the distinctive sound and construction of Gullah to the inability of slaves to master standard English grammar and pronunciation (for example, Crum).[21] Others said it reflected the "baby talk" whites used to communicate with slaves.[22] Turner revealed that the characteristic elements of Gullah reflect both African roots and English dialects of colonial Carolina, similar to the way in which Jamaican *patois* is both African and English. The density of the black population in the low country allowed West African words, grammatical forms, and sentence patterns to remain more dominant than was the case in other parts of the South. Before its speakers were exposed to public education, radio, and television, Gullah was undoubtedly an even more distinctive dialect than it is today.

As documented historically and in this century by Turner, one way in which Africans maintained their linguistic heritage while integrating it with English speech was in the names they used. A colonial plantation owner listed the following among his slaves: *Allahay, Assey, Benyky, Bungey, Colley, Cumbo, Cush, Dusue, Esher, Into, Jehu, Jeminah, Matillah, Meynell, Minto, Quamino, Quash, Quashey, Rinah, Sambo, Satirah, Sibbey, Tehu, Temboy, Tiffey, Yeabow, and Yeackney.*[23] Sometimes the African name was shortened when interacting with whites to more a English-sounding one; thus *Cudjo* became *Joe* and *Quaco* became *Jack.*

Among the words Turner collected were these, which are widely used in the South[25]:

| | |
|---|---|
| *bene* "benne or sesame" | Wolof (Senegal and Gambia) and Bambara (Mali) "the sesame" |
| *bidibidi* "a small bird," "a small chicken" | Kongo (Angola) "a bird" |
| *gombo* "okra" | Tshiluba (Congo) and Umbundu (Angola) "okra" |
| *guba* "peanut" | Kimbundu (Angola) and Umbundu (Angola) "peanut" |
| *juju* "magic, evil spirit" | Hausa (Northern Nigeria) "a fetish, an evil spirit" |

| | |
|---|---|
| *kuta* "tortoise" | Bambara (Mali), Malinke (Ivory Coast), Efik (Southern Nigeria), Djerma (Niger), and Tshiluba (Congo) "tortoise, turtle" |
| *samba* "to dance" | Hausa (Northern Nigeria) "a dance of youths and maidens;" Tshiluba (Congo) "to jump about, to be here and there" |
| *tot* "to carry" | Kikongo (Congo) and Kongo (Angola) "to pick up," Umbundu (Angola) "to carry" |
| *wudu* "witchcraft, sorcery" | Ewe (Togo and Dahomey) "a deity or demon;" Fon (Dahomey) "a good or bad spirit," "an intermediary between God and man," "a deity" |
| *yam* "sweet potato" | Mende (Sierra Leone) "the wild yam" |

Gullah folk stories captured attention early on, because of both the dialect in which they were told and their colorful themes. The stories include fables with well-known animal characters like Brer Rabbit, terrifying ghost tales, and accounts of spiritual experiences. The tales were first widely publicized in the late 19th century by Joel Chandler Harris, who used them as the basis for his Uncle Remus stories. Then they were recorded with varying degrees of dialectic accuracy by many others who followed, including Dubose Heyward, creator of the Gullah characters in *Porgy*, John Bennett,[26] the Georgia Writers' Project of the Work Projects Administration,[27] Elsie Clews Parsons,[28] Ambrose Gonzales,[29] Mason Crum,[30] and Patricia Jones-Jackson.[31] This example, transliterated to make it more understandable to English readers, was collected in the late thirties by the Georgia Writers' Project on Wilmington Island. It gives a sense of the cadence and style of Gullah speech, which would be even more challenging in actual hearing.[32]

> Various members of the party asked Peter McQueen to tell one of the numerous stories about Brer Rabbit and Brer Wolf. Peter pondered for a minute; then he started:
>
> "Bruh Rabbit and Bruh Wolf wuz alluz tryin tuh git duh bes uh one anudduh. Now Bruh Wolf he own a hoe an it

wuk fuh crop all by itsef. Bruh Wolf jis say, 'Swish,' tuh it. Den he sit down in duh fiel an duh hoe do all duh wuk.

"Bruh Rabbit he wahn dat hoe. He hide behine bush an watch how duh wolf make it wuk. One day wen duh wolf way, Bruh Rabbit he steal duh hoe. He go tuh he own fiel an he stan duh hoe up an he say, 'Swish.' Duh hoe staht tuh wuk. It wuk and it wuk. Fo long duh crop is done finish. Den rabbit want hoe tuh stop, an he call out an he call out but hoe keep right on wukin. Bruh Rabbit dohn know wut wud tuh say tuh stop it. Pretty soon duh hoe cut down all Bruh Rabbit wintuh crop an still it keep on wukkin an wukkin. Bruh Rabbit wring he hans. Ebryting he hab is gone. Jis den Bruh Wolf come long an he laugh an he laugh out loud wen he see how Bruh Rabbit steal he hoe an how it done ruin all duh crop. Bruh Rabbit he keep callin out, 'Swish, swish,' an duh hoe go fastuhn fastuh. Wen he see Bruh Wolf, he ax um tuh make duh hoe stop. Bruh wolf wohn say nuttn uhtall cuz he mad dat Bruh Rabbit steal he hoe. Den attuh a time he say, 'Slow, boy,' and duh hoe he stop wukkin. Den Bruh Wolf he pick up he hoe an carry um home."

# Notes

[1]Mason Crum, *Gullah: Negro Life in the Carolina Sea Islands.* (New York: Negro Universities Press, 1968.), p. 42.

[2]Alvin M. Josephy, Jr, *500 Nations; An Illustrated History of North American Indians.* (New York: Alfred A. Knopf, 1994), p. 141.

[3]Peter H. Wood, *Black Majority; Negroes in Colonial South Carolina from 1670 through the Stono Rebellion.* (New York: W.W. Norton and Company, 1975), pp. 3-6.

[4]Wood, p. 21.

[5]Wood, p. 144.

[6]Census data for 1790.

[7]Census data for 1860.

[8]Patricia Jones-Jackson, *When Roots Die; Endangered Traditions on the Sea Islands.* (Athens: University of Georgia Press, 1987), p. 11.

[9]Daniel C. Littlefield, *Rice and Slaves; Ethnicity and the Slave Trade in Colonial South Carolina.* (Urbana and Chicago: University of Illinois Press, 1991), Table 9.

[10]Wood, pp. 334-339.

[11]Littlefield, p. 115.

[12]Littlefield, p. 123.

[13]Lorenzo Dow Turner, *Africanisms in the Gullah Dialect.* (Ann Arbor: University of Michigan Press, 1974), p. 2.

[14]Wood, p. 30.

[15]Wood, p. 60.

[16]Wood, p. 61; Charles Joyner, *Down by the Riverside; A South Carolina Slave Community.* (Urbana: University of Illinois Press, 1984), pp. 45-48.

[17]T.J. Woofter, Jr, *Black Yeomanry; Life on St. Helena Island.* (New York: Henry Holt and Company, 1930), pp. 8-9.

[18]Joyner, p. 46.

[19]Wood, pp. 122-123.

[20]Joyner, pp. 70-71.

[21]Crum, already cited.

[22]Turner, p. 5.

[23]Wood, p. 181.

[24]Wood, p. 182.

[25]Turner, pp. 190-204.

[26]John Bennett, *The Doctor to the Dead; Grotesque Legends and Folk Tales of Old Charleston.* Columbia: University of South Carolina Press, 1995.

[27]Georgia Writers' Project, Work Projects Administration, *Drums and Shadows; Survival Studies Among the Georgia Coastal Negroes.* (Garden City: Anchor Books, 1972).

[28]Elsie Clews Parsons, *Folk-Lore of the Sea Islands, South Carolina.* Cambridge, MA and New York: Memoirs of the American Folk-Lore Society, volume XVI, 1923.

[29]Gonzales, Ambrose E, *The Black Border.* (Columbia: University of South Carolina Press, 1922).

[30]already cited

[31]already cited

[32]Georgia Writers' Project, pp. 103-104.

# Chapter 2

## Sources of Black Folk Medicine in Native America

> The red men of the American forests are never at a loss to know which plant is best, nor the time it should he gathered, to cure them of disease. They know how to treat their complaints in physic, surgery, and midwifery with a skill that far surpasses that of many a learned doctor of the big medical schools, with all their science.[1]

The first doctors encountered by the colonials were native American. To quote Vogel:

> So complete was the aboriginals' knowledge of their native flora that Indian usage can be demonstrated for all but a bare half dozen, at most, of our indigenous vegetable drugs. In a surprising number of instances, moreover, the aboriginal uses of these drugs corresponded with those approved in the Dispensatory of the United States. There is in addition a list of several hundred aboriginal remedies which have been used in domestic medicine as well as by physicians, although they have not won general acceptance.[2]

Those colonials who lived close to native Americans respected their medical expertise and attempted to acquire some of this vast botanical knowledge. The backwoods soon filled with "Indian doctors"—white men who claimed to have acquired their medical knowledge from the native Americans. During the first half of the nineteenth century, the Indian doctors were especially prevalent; they supplied roots, herbs, and the books they had written to far flung and isolated communities, and became important in rural America. Some of the books strongly influenced lay the popularity of Indian medicine were:

Bowker, Pierpont E. *The Indian Vegetable Family Instructor* (1836).
Rogers, Dr. D. *The American Physician* (1824).
Smith, Peter. *The Indian Doctor's Dispensatory, Being Father Smith's Advice Respecting Diseases and Their Cure* (1812).
Sperry, Dr. L. *The Botanic Family Physician, or, The Secret of Curing Diseases* (1843).

Household editions of European medical books were also sold at this time. As would be expected, university-trained doctors resisted the influences of Indian doctors and adhered to European books.

By the mid-nineteenth century, the medicine of the average white American contained elements of both native American and European medical practices. It should be kept in mind that the medical knowledge that the colonials brought from Europe was no more scientific or advanced than native American medicine. Aside from their own prejudices, the settlers would not have had any valid reasons for rejecting native American medicine. In the isolated, harsh circumstances in which most settlers found themselves, moreover, there was no room to pick and choose.

Following are some illustrations of native American and Euro-American folk remedies for common ailments. The Euro-American medicine is the type that would be found in the typical nineteenth-century home medical manual. Bear in mind that these were by no means the only remedies for these complaints.

| *Ailment* | *Native American Remedies* | *Euro-American Remedies* |
|---|---|---|
| Asthma | mullein or jimson weed | licorice root with mullein leaves, horehound, and lungwort |
| Coughs | wild black cherry; seneca; snakeroot | cherry bark with life everlasting, spikenard root, horehound, elecampane, licorice, and honey |
| Bilious complaints | blackberry root; wild bergamot (Sampson's snakeroot) | cherry bark with blood-root, brandy, water, and molasses |
| Dysentery | wild black cherry; seneca; snakeroot; blackberry root | red oak bark with wild cherry bark and blackberry roots |

| | | |
|---|---|---|
| Sores | crushed onions and wild garlic; sweet gum balsam; nightshade | mashed elderberry leaves; powdered comfrey root; powdered bloodroot; fresh pokeroot |

One fact becomes immediately apparent: Whereas native American remedies were composed mostly of one plant, Euro-American folk medicine was characterized by its combination of numerous ingredients into one medicine. Here, just a few examples are given, but the truth of this comparison is borne out by continued investigation.

Euro-American adaptation to American ecology is shown in the use of such indigenous plants as life everlasting, blackberry, pokeroot, and wild black cherry. The last one in particular enjoyed a long popularity, and was at one time the most popular ingredient in home remedies for coughs and colds. Some of the herbs were used for many ailments. Generally, by varying the concentration or method of preparation, the remedy was made more specific for a particular disease or organ of the body.

Native American medicine surely influenced Afro-American folk medicine as well, especially in the Southeast, where the greatest contact occurred between the two races. Since there is no historical record documenting this exchange of knowledge, similar use of roots and herbs by native Americans and Afro-Americans is the best evidence that the exchange took place.

The following chart shows how native Americans and Afro-Americans have used certain roots and herbs similarly, indicating an Afro-American adaptation of native American folk medical treatments. Individual remedies in both native American and Afro-American herbal medicine consisted of just a few plants, three at most, usually brewed with water.

| *Herb* | *Native American Use* | *Afro-American Use* |
|---|---|---|
| Blackberry | stomach pains, diarrhea, and dysentery | stomach pains, diarrhea, and dysentery |
| Life everlasting | swollen glands | cramps, fever, and toothache |
| Pine tar | inflammation, burns, sore throat, and colds | colds, fever, and spring tonic |
| Sampson's snakeroot | stomach pain and backache | indigestion |

# Notes

1 Dr. O. Phelps Brown, *The Complete Herbalist, or The People Their Own Physicians, by the Use of Nature's Remedies, Describing the Great Curative Properties Found in the Herbal Kingdom* (Jersey City, N.J.: published by the author, 1874), p. 15.

2 Virgil J. Vogel, *American Indian Medicine* (Norman: University of Oklahoma Press, 1970), p. 6.

*Dune grasses and palmetto palms along the coast.*

# Chapter 3

## Sources of Black Folk Medicine on the Plantation

The extent to which Euro-American folk medicine influenced that of Afro-Americans is difficult to determine. The interchange, regardless of the degree to which it occurred, took place primarily in the southern states. This chapter begins with some examples of black folk medicine in the antebellum urban South. The second section of the chapter examines the medical care of black plantation slaves. Descriptions of the plantation experience are analyzed to determine the degree to which plantation medical care hindered or aided the development of black folk medicine.

In the 1700s, the following news item appeared in the *Carolina Gazette*, concerning a black named Caesar:

> The General Assembly has purchased the negro Caesar's freedom and granted him a pension of 100 pounds per annum during life, as a reward for the discovery of the means by which he acquired so much celebrity in curing persons who had swallowed poison or been bitten by a rattlesnake.[1]

Another slave, named Sampson, cured snakebite with the root that still bears his name in the Sea Islands and other areas.[2]

These are just two examples that testify to the fact that, from an early period, Afro-Americans were involved in health-related activities. This involvement is also reflected in a law passed in 1749 by the General Assembly of South Carolina that prohibited slaves, under threat of death, from employment by physicians or apothecaries, expressly so that slaves could not concoct poisons or administer medicines of any kind.[3] A slave could also be whipped up to 50 strokes for administering "any medicine, or pretended medicine, to any other slave" except under the supervision of a white person.[4] A contemporary opinion sheds some light on this ruling. Writing from Charleston in 1750 to Charles Alston, who had been his teacher, Alexander Garden stated that, in fact, physicians frequently used the diagnosis of poisoning to cover their ignorance of the real cause of illness.[5] It is evident, then, that the 1749 act was a product of ignorance, compounded with fear and suspicion. Doubtless, however, certain blacks, given the opportunity, did poison their masters. In any event, these attempts at suppression notwithstanding, black knowledge and use of natural medicines continued unabated until modern times, as the text to follow fully illustrates.

Waring has stated, in *A History of Medicine in South Carolina*, that

> the medical care of the slave was in general as good as that of his master and better than that of the lower class white man. On all the larger plantations hospitals were provided and medical and nursing care was made available, often at large expense. In simple cases of disease the planter-physician or his overseer made efforts at treatment, but for serious illness the services of the real practitioner or attendant or consultant were required regularly.[6]

In fact, masters who maintained satisfactory medical facilities for the treatment of disease were the exception rather than the rule. Fanny Kemble's description of a hospital on a typical Georgia rice and cotton plantation is summarized by Kenneth Stampp:

> The floors were "merely the hard damp earth itself," most of the windows were unglazed, the rooms were dirty and malodorous, and the inmates "lay prostrate on the floor, without bed, mattress, or pillow, buried in tattered and filthy blankets." Sick and well alike were "literally encrusted with dirt" and infested with "swarms of fleas." ... A condition of more complete indifference toward the invalids and disregard for the most elementary roles of sanitation could scarcely he imagined.[7]

The average slave master was fairly ignorant of the importance of good health measures; many limited medical expenditures for the sake of economy. Except in the most severe cases, these masters and overseers made their own diagnoses and prescribed remedies without the aid of the doctor, who was employed as infrequently as possible. The master and his wife, with the assistance of female slaves, or the overseer alone, treated the ailing slaves. Their knowledge was drawn from popular magazines, medical books written specifically for the planter, or their own home remedies. One volume, *The Planter's and Mariner's Medical Companion*, was written specifically to fill the needs of the slave owner. The *Charleston Medical Journal* and the *Popular Medicine* magazine also presented articles of interest to planters. Masters frequently refused to treat ailing slaves until they were visibly ill. Until then the owners often suspected that the slaves were feigning sickness to escape work. On the other hand, the complete neglect of ailing slaves by overseers was a major complaint of more responsible slave owners. Under these conditions it is clear why the slaves maintained their own medical practices, especially to cure everyday illnesses.

As far as the efficacy of antebellum medicine itself was concerned, Stampp states:

> Unfortunately, the state of antebellum medical science made it uncertain that even the most conscientious master would invariably prescribe better remedies than the...slave healer...Diseased slaves who received [antebellum] remedies...could have counted themselves fortunate if the remedies did not retard recovery or hasten death.[8]

Stampp also notes this entry from a plantation diary:

> A Louisiana slave took a dose of a "Tonic Mixture" prescribed by a respected physician; an hour later he told his master that he felt very strange, as if his insides were coming up, as if the tip of his head were coming off. He soon died.[9]

Another aspect of southern medicine that could have complicated treatment was the general belief among southern whites that blacks were not of the same species as whites. Believed to differ both anatomically and physiologically, it was thought they might require special medical treatment. Most physicians, however, did not put these theories into practice, although one doctor argued that remedies that would cure a white man might injure or even kill a black.[10]

Although the practice of medicine by blacks was forbidden by law, some black men and women did function in an official medical position on some plantations. As previously mentioned, female slaves assisted the master's wife, and slave midwives also handled obstetrical cases. On one Georgia plantation a certain slave woman was the "Doctress of the Plantation. In case of extraordinary illness, when she thinks she can do no more for the sick, you will employ a physician."[11]

Most often, slaves probably self-treated their medical problems and only asked for help from the planter or plantation doctor if their remedies failed. African pharmacological traditions were handed down to subsequent generations of slaves by oral tradition, and the flora and fauna of West Africa and the Carolina coast although not unlike were similar enough that a great deal of plant and animal knowledge was transferable.[12] In addition, the Indians with whom the Africans came into contact shared their knowledge of local wildlife.

Slaves who were specialists in healing others with herbs and roots were themselves commonly called "doctors" (or doctress). Handing down their knowledge from generation to generation, these "doctors" were generally conversant not only with natural medicines for everyday acute and chronic conditions, but also with magical medicines for treating special problems, and toxins that could be used for benign purposes like poisoning fish or more aggressively to kill other people. Magical medicines, akin to voodoo in Louisiana, used animal parts like feathers, blood, and bones, human substances like hair clippings and fingernails, and other natural substances like leaves, sand, and water to cure problems that appeared to be caused by other people's magic, to put spells on people, to attract love and money, and so forth. Magical practices were feared and suppressed by whites, and were kept hidden from them. Likewise, the "doctors" kept their knowledge of plant poisons hidden, because of the risks of punishment.

Margaret Slack, an ex-slave interviewed in Georgia, said of the plantation on which she lived, "The Negroes received care and treatment during illness from their fellow-slaves or from their 'white folks'"[13] Some blacks were consulted by blacks and whites alike on medical matters. Another writer, Meyer, has stated unequivocally that "slaves doctored themselves. Like the Indians they had always lived close to nature and quickly learned the properties of plants."[14]

The preceding discussion concerned the South in general. Given the isolation and size of the Sea Islands plantations, it is obvious that the slaves were responsible for their own medical care. As mentioned, during the "sickly season"—the hot, damp, summer months—few South Carolina planters remained on their land. They fled from the malaria-infested islands in May and did not return until the first frost in the fall. The overseers of these temporarily or permanently absentee landlords were the only white men who were encountered on these plantations. It goes without saying that one overseer—even if he knew much about medicine—could hardly tend to the medical needs of a large group of people.

Some of the reasons for the survival of black folk medicine through the antebellum era have been made clear. That a separate black folk medicine was recognized even then is reflected in the repeated references made in literature written during the plantation period to herbal medicines used only by blacks. Such references may be found it the writings of Byrd (1709), Porcher (1849), and other authors. Many are reproduced in the second section of the book.

A look at the typical medicines prescribed by nineteenth-century planters' manuals will give an idea of the differences between this medicine and black folk herb remedies. The principal illnesses treated were: malaria, yellow fever, cholera, tuberculosis, pneumonia, typhoid, tetanus, dysentery, colds, influenza, scarlet fever, whooping cough, chicken pox, smallpox, typhus, snakebite, and "occupational disorders."[15] *The Medical Vade Mecum*, a popular planter's medical book of the early nineteenth century, recommended for these illnesses such medicines as: sulfur, magnesia, paregoric antimony, rhubarb, powder of tin, and calomel.

A prescription account book of a South Carolina plantation lists calomel, opium, ipecac, Dover's powders, sugar of lead, camphor, and snakeroot tea as therapeutic agents. Other substances used by planters were: quinine, bitter apple, laudanum, cream of tartar, wild cherry, blue moss, whiskey and arsenic. Physicians, planters, and overseers also generously patronized the patent medicine manufacturers.

Most of the substances used by the planters and overseers were chemical substances derived from plants, rather than, as is typical of Sea Islands medicine, decoctions, infusions, or teas made from parts of the living plant. Of the sample lists, only snakeroot, bitter apple, and wild cherry can he found in contemporary Sea Islands medicine.

Despite the apparent differences, however, plantation medicine certainly influenced black folk medicine. By the same token, black herb medicine certainly influenced white folk medicine, since blacks doctored whites as well as other blacks. Unfortunately, we cannot directly trace the history of black folk medicine through the years of enslavement. We have seen, however, how the plantation medical system ensured its continued existence.

## Notes

[1]Clarence Meyer, *American Folk Medicine* (New York: Thomas Y. Crowell Co., 1973), p. 2.

[2]Ibid.

[3]Meyer, p. 3.

[4]Wood, p. 290.

[5]Dr. Joseph Ioor Waring, *A History of Medicine in South Carolina, 1670-1825.* 2 vols. (Charleston: South Carolina Medical Association, 1964-67), 1:225.

[6]Ibid., 2:5.

[7]Kenneth M. Stampp, *The Peculiar Institution: Slavery in the Ante-Bellum South* (New York: Vintage Books, 1956), pp.317-18. From the journal of Fanny Kemble, who was a planter's wife.

[8]Ibid., pp. 279-321.

[9]Ibid., p. 308. From the diary of William J. Minor, entry for Sept.24, 1857.

[10]Ibid., p. 309.

[11]Ibid., p.306. From the records of Telfair Plantation.

[12]Wood, p. 120.

[13]William Dosite Postell, *The Health of Slaves on Southern Plantations* (Baton Rouge: Louisiana State University Press, 1951), p.108.

[14]Meyer, *American Folk Medicine,* p.3.

[15]Postell, *The Health of Slaves,* pp. 74-89.

# Chapter 4

## The Traditional Black Medical System

Throughout the New World, black folk medicine divides illnesses and their treatment into three categories, the particular category being determined by the cause of illness. The system distinguishes between those illnesses that are natural in origin, those spiritual in origin, and those caused by occult powers.

### Natural Illnesses

Natural illnesses are those brought about by the weather, cold air, and similar natural forces. These illnesses are cured with roots, herbs, barks, and teas, by an *herbalist*—an individual skilled in the use of natural therapeutic substances. The materials used by the herbalist are termed *medicine* or *roots*. Strictly speaking, the term "roots" should apply only to natural materials. In fact, its meaning had been extended with time to include both natural and occult medicines. Sea Islands herbal medicine belongs to this category of treatment. Its materials consist of barks, berries, roots, leaves, and herbs, and the treatment is reserved for those illnesses brought about by natural elements. The home remedies used by blacks throughout the South belong to the category of natural healing substances.

### Occult Illnesses

The technique by which supernatural forces or agents produce illness is called *hoodoo*, *conjure*, or *ju-ju*. The individual suffering from a hoodoo-caused illness has been *crossed* or *hexed*. Several factors distinguish hex illnesses from those caused by natural sources. The main distinction is in the origin of the illness. In hoodoo, the *conjurer* uses his or her own powers, as well as those invested in certain words, materials, and objects, to produce illness in specific individuals. The client names the individual who will be hexed, as well as the type of hex to be used.

The person who has been hexed frequently exhibits behavioral as well as organic symptoms. Thus, he or she may behave in an asocial or "insane" manner and suffer from head or stomach pains as well. The hex need not result in any organic symptoms, however. Crossing may produce bad luck, loss of a job, or a strong desire to leave town. Thus, while natural causes produce only physical illnesses, hoodoo can affect many areas of life adversely. However, a hoodoo *amulet* or *hand* will protect the wearer financially and occupationally, as well as medically.

A person who has been crossed will not recover fully until the spell has been removed. This also can be done only by a conjurer. Natural illnesses, on the other hand, can he cured by an herbalist, home remedies, or a clinical treatment. Conjurers are usually skilled in the use of herbal cures as well as in occult methods. A person who is both herbalist and conjurer is frequently called a *root doctor*, and the terms roots and root medicine include hoodoo as well as herbs.

## Spiritual Illnesses

Those illnesses caused by sin or the devil fall within the category of spiritual illnesses. Like the forces of the occult, spiritual sources can produce misfortune as well as physical illness. Thus, illness, poor family relations, lack of a good job, and bad luck—frequently occurring together—are all thought to result from spiritual poverty. Though healing may involve such techniques as laying on of hands, anointment, or a verbal blessing, it is must importantly spiritual. The power of God, acting through a religious healer, produces health and happiness in the patient through spiritual renewal. By this renewal, sins are cleansed and the devil's influences are cast out. Spiritual illnesses are most fully cured by religious healers capable of channeling the healing powers of God.

---

The external symptoms of natural, spiritual, and occult illnesses are frequently indistinguishable. For this reason, a sick person may go to a series of practitioners before attaining relief. The search for treatment is aided, however, by the frequent overlap in the roles of practitioners. Thus, a conjurer may also be a herbalist, and a preacher may also be able to cure hexes.

A practitioner may acquire knowledge in three ways: apprenticeship under an established practitioner, heredity, or the "call." The herbalist has generally served an apprenticeship or learned about herbs from a relative. In the Sea Islands, the majority of those knowledgeable in herbs are older women who learned the art from even older female relatives. Spiritual healers and conjurers have usually received a call to healing. Such a gift of healing—whether given at birth or later in life—is believed more powerful than healing learned through apprenticeship.

*Rustic old house on Edisto Island.*

*A Victorian cottage on Wadmalaw Island.*

# Chapter 5

## Contemporary Herb Use

Like many southern communities, the Sea Islands are in the midst of cultural transition. Patterns that have changed little for hundreds of years are beginning to fade. Traditional herbal medicine is one of these. Younger people, although able to name five or six herbs, do not usually know their uses. Knowledgeable older men and women, on the other hand, are aware of the uses of at least fifteen to twenty plants. Increasingly accessible "orthodox" medicine, combined with growing urban influences have made herbal medicine seem old-fashioned and "country."

A decade ago, children were treated more often with herbs than with prescription medicine. Today, older adults make the most use of herbal remedies, especially when medication given by the doctor does not seem to be working. The older people I talked to were unanimous in the belief that traditional methods of healing were the best.

*Wadmalaw Island, 1974.*

*A grove of young sweet gum trees.*

# Directory

## of Sea Islands Medicinal Roots and Herbs

### General Information on Gathering Herbs

There is a certain season when it is best to pick a plant: the time of gathering should coincide with the period when the medical properties of the plant are at their peak.

The roots of annual plants yield their most active properties just before the flowering season, in the early spring. In late fall, when growth has ceased and nutrients for the winter are being stored, roots of biennial and perennial plants should be gathered.

Herbaceous stems should he collected after the foliage has developed and before the flowers have blossomed. Bark should be gathered in the spring before flowering or in the autumn after the foliage has disappeared. Leaves should be gathered between flowering and the maturation of fruit or seeds.

Flowers, buds, and leaves should be gathered in dry weather and dried away from dampness.

### Preparing Remedies

Like Indian medicines, Sea Islands herbal remedies are composed of a few plants, brewed generally with water. A distinguishing characteristic of Euro-American herbal medicine, even when it is derived from Indian medicine, is the use of complicated formulas and mixtures. Frequently five or six different plants are used, rarely one or two.

In native American and Sea Islands medicine alike, the great majority of medicines employ one or two plants, three at most. Perhaps this is indicative of a more exact knowledge of the nature and function of each plant.

The author cannot guarantee the results from using any of the following medicines or be responsible for their effects on individuals.

## Key to Directory

The information in the directory appears in this order:

Description of the plant.

Medicinal part or parts used on Sea Islands.

Medicinal use on Sea Islands.

Officially recognized properties. (The initials *USP* stood for *The United States Pharmacopeia*. The initials NF stand for *The National Formulary*.)

Use by other Afro-Americans.

Use by native Americans.

Use by Euro-Americans.

## ALOE, AMERICAN

*Agave virginica*

Description: Thick, long, succulent leaves. Blooms throughout summer months. Found in sandy and open woods from Virginia to Florida.

Part used: Leaves.

Use: "Called by the negroes Rattlesnake's master. A domestic remedy for flatulent colic; used in Charleston for the bite of the rattlesnake."[1]

Euro-American use: Diuretic.[2]

## ANGELICA TREE

(Hercules Club)
*Aralia spinosa*

Description: Large, alternate leaves. May have scattered prickles. Fruits are black berries. Grows into a large shrub or small tree 10 to 20 feet high. Frequently abundant in old clearings or old forest land.

Part used: Root bark.

Use: "In South Carolina, this plant is the rattlesnake's master, par excellence, according to the negroes; they rely on it almost exclusively as a remedy for the bite of serpents. We are informed that they use the bark of the fresh root in substance, taken internally, also applying it powdered to the wounded part."[3] More than one plant was given the name "rattlesnake's master."

Euro-American use: Stimulant; for chronic rheumatism and cutaneous eruptions.[4]

## ARTICHOKE, JERUSALEM

*Helianthus tuberosus*

Description: A native American sunflower. Its thick and fleshy rootstock bears edible tubers. Has a very rough, hairy stem 6 to 10 feet tall. Leaves are thick, hard, and large. Flowers are yellow. The plant grows in moist thickets and open places.

Part used: Leaves.

Use: "Great use is made of it on the plantations in this state [South Carolina] as a tonic and diuretic in dropsy; the leaves are steeped in rum…among the negroes we have frequently seen it prescribed with advantage in this way. It is employed also in jaundice."[5]

Native American use: Tubers eaten as food.

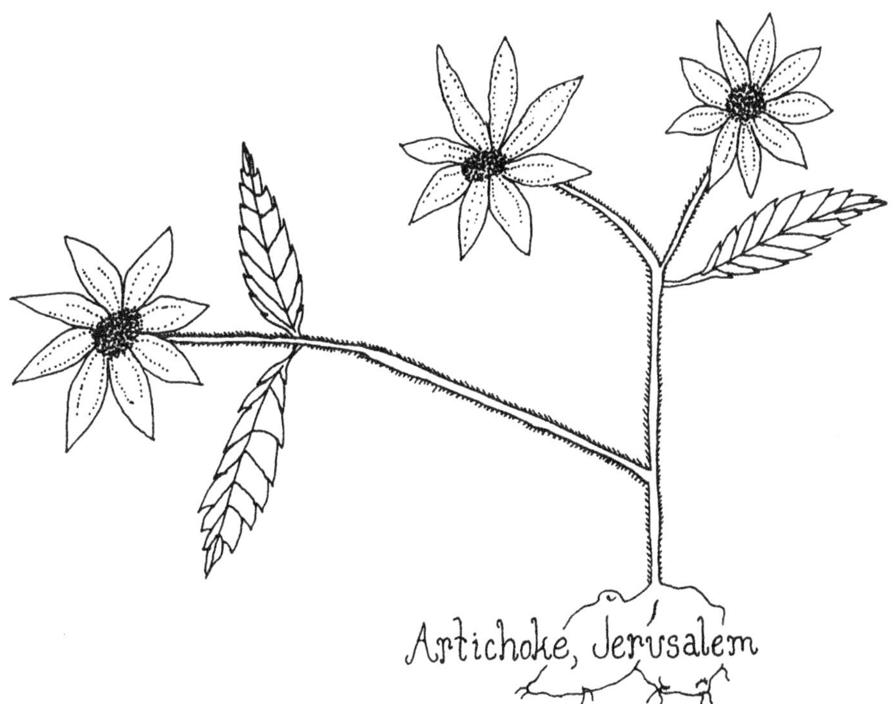

## AYSHABERRY

(Black Cohosh or Black Snakeroot)
*Cimicifuga racemosa*

Description: Slender stem from 3 to 6 feet tall, on which grow 2 or 3 large, compound leaves. Leaflets are sharply toothed on margin. Flowers are large, white tassels. The leaves are said to drive away bugs, hence the name: cimex, a bug, and fuge, to drive away.

Part used: Leaves.

Use: Chew or boil leaf for relief of worms in animals or people.

Other Afro-American use: Chills, fever.[6]

Native American use: Colds, pneumonia.[7]

Euro-American use: Tonic for mucous tissues; also as narcotic and sedative.[8]

*In Georgia:* Colic.[9]

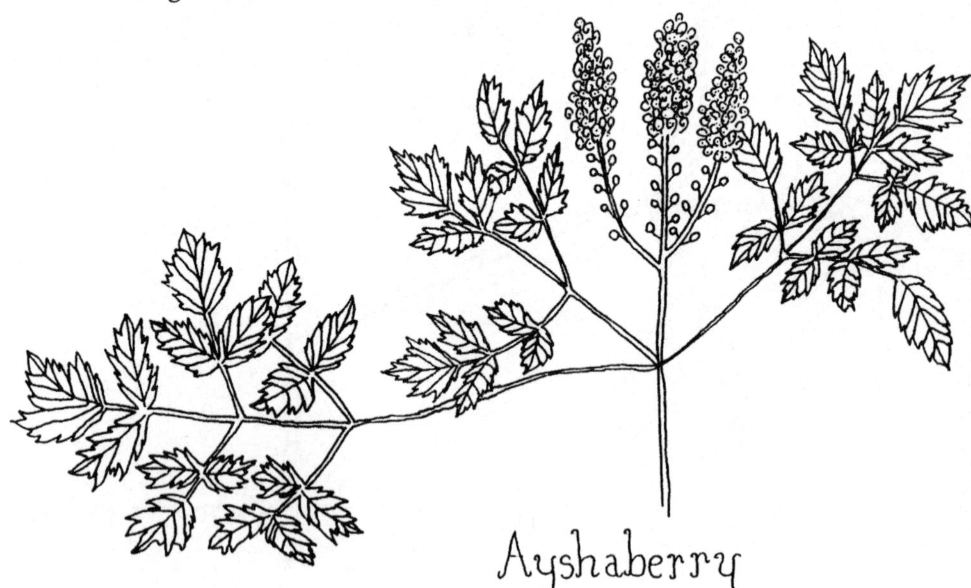

## BITTER APPLE

*Cucumis colocynthis*

Description: An annual plant with lobed leaves, hairy on the underside. Has yellow flowers, smooth fruit. "Apple" is the size of an orange, yellow when ripe, with a thin, solid rind and very bitter flesh. A native of Southern Europe, Africa, and Asia.

Part used: Fruit with rind removed.

Use: Fever.

Euro-American use: Fruit commonly dried in stove or by sun. Used as powerful cathartic, sometimes in conjunction with black henbane.[10]

## BLACKBERRY

*Rubus*

Description: A trailing plant with slender branches. The stems are covered with sharp thorns. Flowers are white, fruit is black and edible. Grows in sandy or dry soil. Indigenous to the United States.

Part used: Root.

Use: Griping in the stomach; general stomach pains.

Official use: The dried bark of the rhizome and roots of the genus *Rubus* was official in the *USP* from 1820 to 1916 and in the *NF* from 1916 to 1936 as an astringent and tonic.[11]

Other Afro-American use: Dysentery and diarrhea—brew tea.[12]
Native American use: Diarrhea, dysentery; poultice against pneumonia; diuretic; relief of stomach trouble.[13]

Euro-American use: Diarrhea, cholera, dysentery.[14]
*In Louisiana*: Stomach cramps.[15]
*In Georgia:* Dysentery.[16]

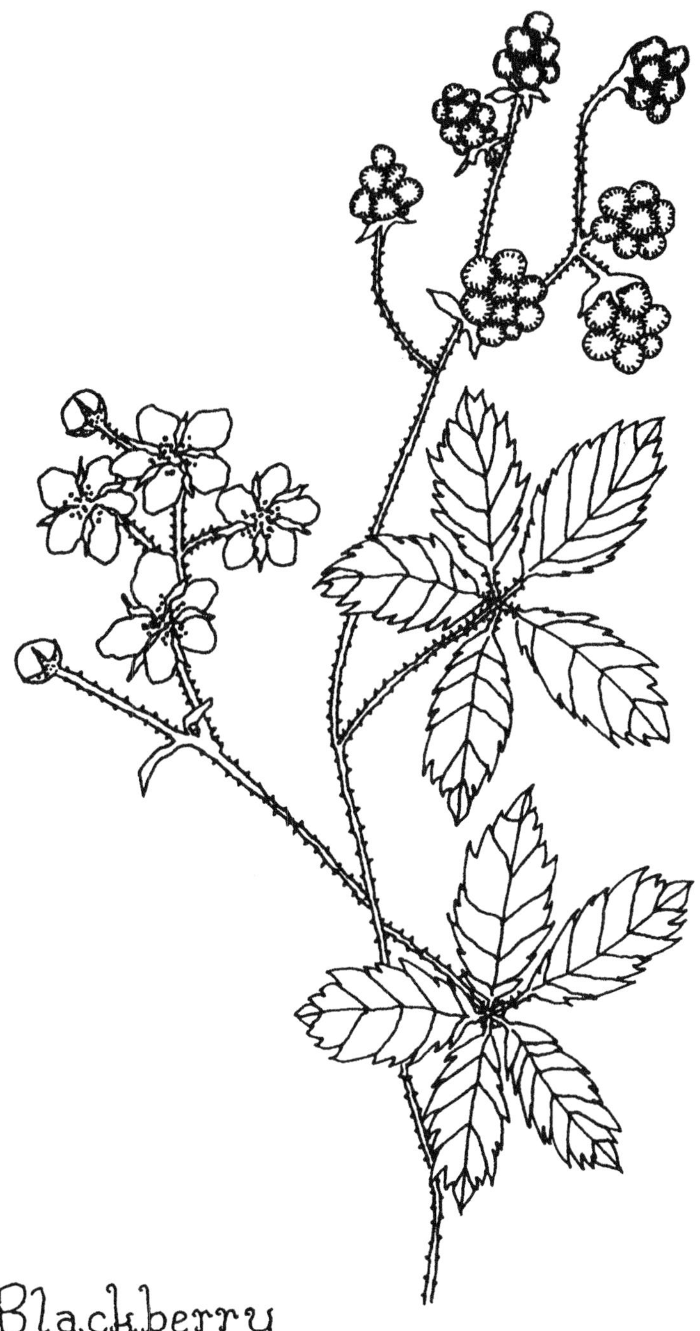

Blackberry

## BLACKROOT

*Pterocaulon pycnostachyum*

Description: Is 2 to 3 feet tall, has simple stem with lance-shaped leaves. The undersides of the leaves, the stem, and the flower cluster are densely coated with felted, whitish wool. The upper surfaces of the leaves are bright green. The name is derived from the thick, black root. One of the unique and striking plants found in the moist parts of the coastal plains wetlands.

Part used: Root.

Use: Body and confinement colds—drink tea made from root.

Other Afro-American use: "Much use is made of this plant (Pterocaulon Pycnostachyum) in St. John's...as an alterative; it is supposed to be possessed of decided value. It is well known as the blackroot of the negroes."[17]

## BLOODROOT

(Redroot)
*Ceanothus ovatus*

Description: A low shrub. Leaves are egg shaped and blunt tipped, smooth above and velvety beneath. Grows to 4 feet high. Although nonleguminous, nitrogen-fixing modules appear on roots. Abundant in the United States, especially in dry woodlands.

Part used: Bark of the root.

Use: Boil the bark of the root and drink the tea to relieve poor circulation.

Official use: Closely related to *Ceanothus americanus* (New Jersey tea), the root of which contains a large amount of prussic acid, of which ceanothine is the active principle.[18]

Other Afro-American use: "To prevent conception, brew 'black law' roots, drop in bluestone, strain and bottle. In another bottle place bloodroot tea mixed with red pepper and tsp. of gunpowder. Every time the moon changes, take a little from each bottle and you will be childless forever."[19]
Dragon's blood—redroot fibers are crushed for multipurpose conjuring and protection.[20]

Euro-American use: Close relative of New Jersey tea, used as astringent, expectorant, sedative, antispasmodic. Used in dysentery, asthma, bronchitis, whooping cough, consumption, sore mouth, and sore throat.[21]

## BONESET

*Eupatorium perfoliatum*

Description: A perennial. Rough, hairy stems 1 to 5 feet high, white and numerous flowers. Very bitter taste. Indigenous to the United States, ranging as far west as Texas and Nebraska. Grows on low ground, on the borders of swamps and streams.

Parts used: Tops and leaves.

Use: "The plant is extensively employed among the negroes on the plantations in this State [South Carolina] as a tonic and diaphoretic in colds and fevers, and in the typhoid pneumonia so prevalent among them."[22]

Euro-American use: Emetic, tonic, laxative; for rheumatism, catarrh, dropsy, typhoid pneumonia.[23] Called boneset because it was supposed that its use caused rapid union of broken bones.

## CHERRY, WILD BLACK

*Prunus serotina*

Description: Medium-sized to large tree, 50 to 60 feet high. Grows in both deep, moist, fertile soil and sandy soil. Fruits used for wine and jelly.

Part used: Bark.

Use: A tea made from the bark relieves arthritic pains.

Official use: The dried bark has been listed with the *USP* continually since 1820. All parts of this plant yield hydrocyanic acid when steeped in water. The medical properties of the bark are destroyed in boiling, so the plant should soak only in warm water.[24]

Other Afro-American use: Tea from cherry tree bark, taken cold, will stop the menstrual flow almost at once.[25] Syrup for sore throat—wild cherry bark, hickory bark, and horehound leaves. Boil down and add sugar to make syrup.[26]

Native American use: Syrup for colds, pains of childbirth, pains and soreness in chest, diarrhea. Poultice for wounds and sores. To make eye wash—soak bark in water.[27]

Euro-American use: The bark of the wild cherry was at one time the most popular ingredient in home remedies for coughs and colds. It was combined with bloodroot, brandy, water, and molasses for bilious complaints, and mixed with certain other barks for a blood purifier.[28]

*In Georgia:* Tonic for blood—wild cherry bark, sweet gum, and mullein, boiled down and mixed with honey.[29]

## CLAY

Description: Red or blue clay from a creek or any other muddy place, such as a hog pen, is used.

Part used: Entire substance.

Use: Sprains—clay may be used alone on the sprain, in the form of a poultice, or mixed with vinegar or vinegar and green Spanish moss.

Other Afro-American use: Rheumatism—vinegar and clay poultice;[30] stings—clay and chewing tobacco.[31]

Euro-American use: Sprains—apply mud poultice.[32]
*In Georgia:* Sprains—poultice of clay and vinegar.[33]

## COMFREY

*Symphytum officinale*

Description: A low, perennial plant with large, hairy, green leaves. The root is oblong and fleshy, the flowers are pale and white. A native of Europe, comfrey was naturalized in the United States. It grows in low grounds and moist places.

Part used: Leaves.

Use: A tea made from the leaves will relieve body pains of a general nature.

Euro-American use: The root was the part used. Comfrey was advised for pulmonary affections, bronchitis, colds, diarrhea, dysentery, leucorrhea, painful swellings, tumors, sores, and bruises.[34]

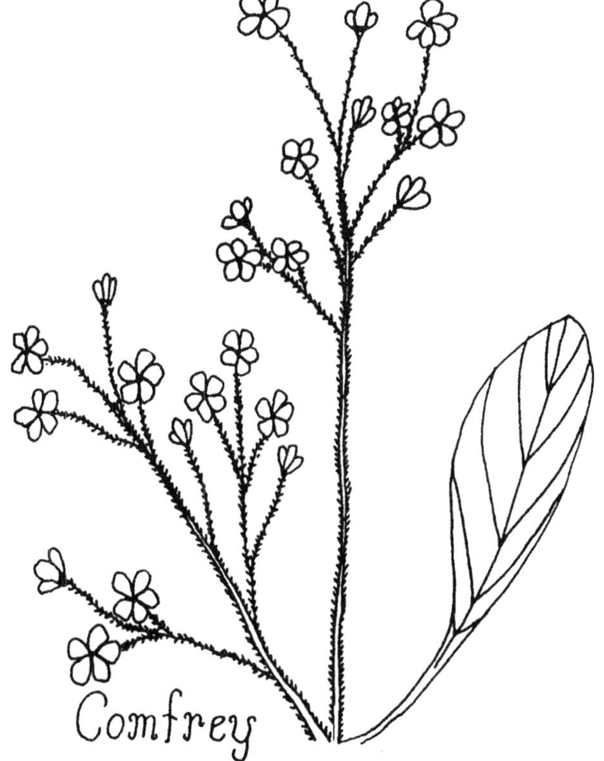

## COTTON

*Gossypium herbaceum*

Description: A biennial or triennial herb, with a round, branching stem about 5 feet high. Hairy, palm-shaped leaves and yellow flowers. The fruit is a 3- or 5-celled capsule in which the seeds are embedded. Originally native to Asia, cotton is now cultivated throughout the world.

Part used: The inner bark of a young root.

Use: Chew root to stimulate sexual organs.

Official use: The root bark of this plant was officially recognized in the *USP* from 1863 to 1916 for its effects on the uterine organs. In the nineteenth century the active principle was called "gossypiin."[35]

Other Afro-American use: In 1840 a French writer, Bouchelle, reported that the root bark of cotton was widely used by Negro slaves in America to induce abortion. According to John U. Lloyd, "the credit for the discovery of its uses [as an abortifacent] must be given to the Negroes of the South."[36]

Native American use: To ease labor, small doses were given to aid uterine contractions in childbirth. To relieve labor pains, asthma; to induce abortion.[37]

Euro-American use: Used instead of ergot in cases of difficult labor; for uterine inflammation, sterility, vaginitis, menstrual irregularities. It was believed that the seeds possessed properties that prevented menstruation.[38]

Cotton (Sea Islands)

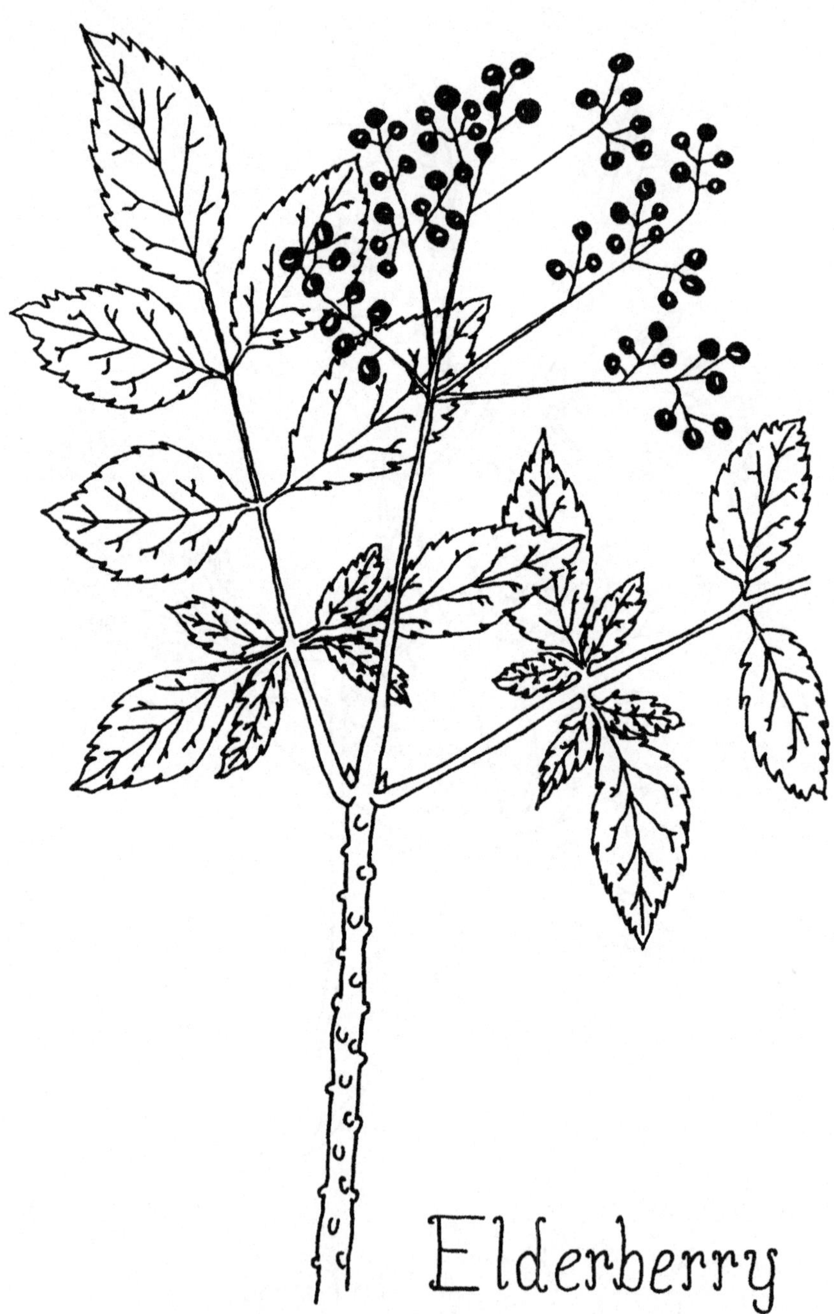
Elderberry

## ELDERBERRY

*Sambucus canadensis*

Description: The elderberry is 5 to 12 feet high, with numerous white flowers. The European elder is similar, but much larger. Grows in low, damp ground and in thickets. Native to the United States.

Parts used: Flowers, berries, inner bark, and root.

Use: The leaves are brewed and the liquid applied externally for the relief of sores.

Official use: Elderberries were official in the *USP* from 1820 to 1831. The flowers were official in the *USP* from 1831 to 1905 and in the *NF* from 1916 to 1947.[39]

Other Afro-American use: For boils—apply a poultice of mashed elderberry leaves.[40]
*In South Carolina:* To relieve chigger bites—apply elderberry flowers stewed in lard.[41]

Native American use: Pain killer; relief from ague, inflammation, headache, colic, and fever.[42]

Euro-American use: Probably because of widespread native American usage, elder became an important ingredient in home remedies. It was used to treat wounds, colds, liver and bowel diseases, "debilities," and as a laxative.[43]

*In Georgia:* For rheumatism—drink elderberry tea or blackberry root tea and rub the area with rattlesnake oil.[44]

## FENNEL

(Dog Fennel)
*Helenium amarum*

Description: A smooth plant with a slender, many-branched stem that is 6 inches to 2 feet tall with very numerous, narrow leaves. Yellow flowers. Grows in meadows, in old fields, and along roads. Indigenous to the United States and common in the Southeast.

Part used: Whole plant.

Use: To take the pain from stings, pull a plant up from the ground and bend it into 3 or 4 sections without breaking it. Holding the sections together, briskly rub the affected area.

Other Afro-American use: To prevent conception and produce abortion—drink dogwood tea, then chew dog-fennel root and swallow the juice.[45] For relief of chills and fever—drink fennel tea.[46]

*In South Carolina:* To stop hiccups and stay thin—drink fennel tea.[47]

Euro-American use: Described as carminative and stimulant, recommended for colic, griping, and spasms. Boil in barley water to increase milk in nursing mother.[48]

*In Georgia:* Drink dog fennel tea for chills, fever, vomiting, and dysentery.[49]

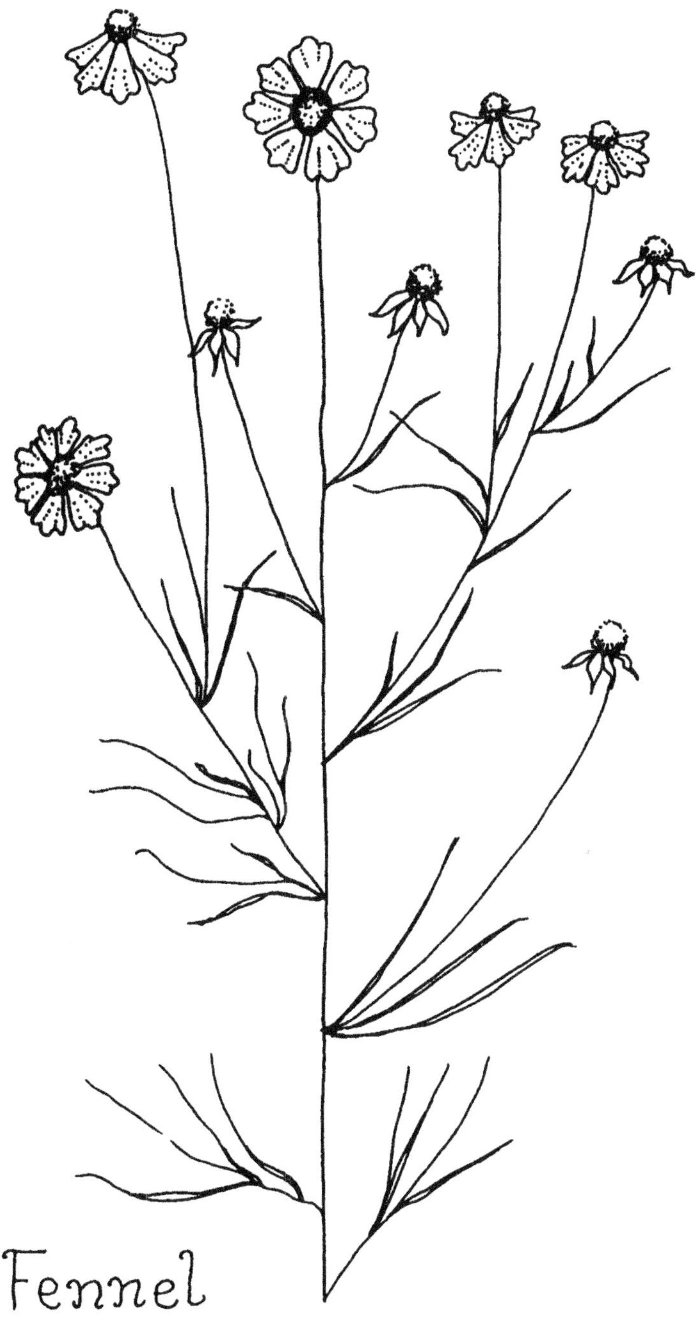
Fennel

## GALAX

(Wild Leek)
*Allium tricoccum*

Description: Another American plant is also called galax. The Sea Islands name refers to a variety of wild leek. In the early spring, the plant has broad, long, flat leaves. After the leaves have withered in June or July, it sends up a naked stalk bearing a crown of greenish white flowers at the top. Wild leek grows in rich, moist woodlands. It is of the same family as wild onion and garlic.

Part used: Bulb.

Use: High blood pressure—there are two methods of use: (1) boil the galax root and drink the resulting liquid, or (2) steep the galax in vinegar or water. Caution must be exercised not to drink too much, so that the blood pressure will not drop too far. Shortness of breath—fry the galax in vaseline and rub the chest with the salve. Small amounts of the salve may also be swallowed.

Official use: The European species of garlic was official in the *USP* from 1820 to 1905 and in the *NF* from 1916 to 1936.[50]

Native American use: For stings, colds (onion syrup), relief of pain from insect stings.[51]

Euro-American use: Onion or garlic juice was used for croup, to rid the bowels of parasites, and to aid digestion.[52]

Galax

## GUM, SWEET
*Liquidambar*

Description: A tall forest dweller, sweet gum is one of the most beautiful of native American trees. It has a very rough bark and short, gray branches with corky ridges. The leaves are shaped like a palm, smooth and shiny. The fruit is round and spiky. Grows in moist areas.

Part used: Leaves.

Use: Sores—dry the leaf, burn it, and place the powdered ash on the sores. Stomach ache—wash the leaf and chew it.

Official use: If the bark of the gum tree is bruised or punctured, a balsam is secreted. This gum balsam was first entered in the *USP* in 1926 and is still officially recognized as an antiseptic agent.[53]

Other Afro-American use: Colds—make a tea from the fruit of the sweet gum tree.[54]

Native American use: For antiseptic purposes.[55]

Euro-American use: In the nineteenth century the medical properties of the gum balsam and the bark were important. The balsam was used for catarrh, coughs, and fever sores; the bark for dysentery and summer complaint. Gum bark, blackberry root, and slippery elm were used in combination for bowel troubles.[56]
*In Georgia:* Burn salve—sweet gum bark, lard, and balm of gilead buds.[57]

## HOLLY

*Ilex*

Description: The term holly may refer to any of a number of bushes that may be found in the swampy, sandy soils of the Southeast. They are characterized by smooth leaves that are usually finely toothed.

Part used: Leaves.

Use: Fever—boil the leaves with pine tar and drink.

Other Afro-American use: Holly leaf tea to bring out measles spots and hasten recovery.[58]

Euro-American use: For colds and coughs. The berries were used as an emetic; the leaves, infused, were prescribed for catarrh, pleurisy, and smallpox.[59]

Gum, Sweet

## HORSENETTLE

*Cnidoscolus stimulosus*

Description: A branching plant 6 inches to 2 feet high, covered with bristlelike and stinging hairs. Leaves have 3 or 5 long, deep lobes. Has long, deep root. Grows in dry, sandy pine lots, fields, and sandhills. Indigenous to the United States.

Part used: Root.

Use: Aphrodisiac. The horsenettle can be chewed alone or it can be combined with blackroot, black pepper, and bloodroot for a powerful effect. The use of this plant was reported as early as 1849: "It possesses some reputation among the negroes in this state [South Carolina], as an aphrodisiac." Plants of this variety are considered "bad roots."[60]

Euro-American use: In nineteenth-century America, horsenettle was used for hemorrhages, diarrhea, dysentery, urinary infections, fever, ague, and asthma.[61]

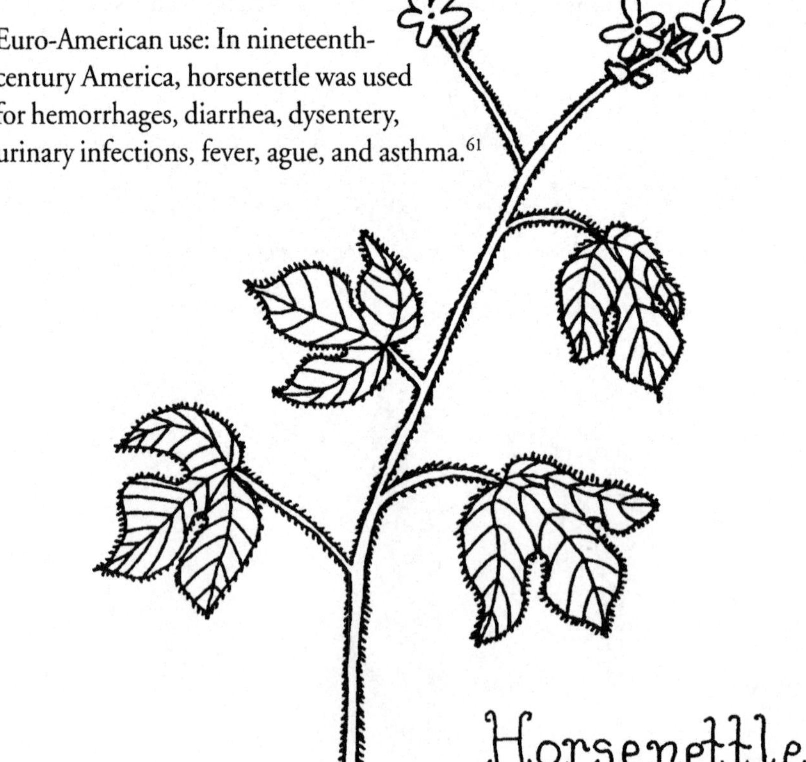

## INDIAN SHOT

(Lady's Slipper)
*Cypripedium acaule*

Description: The lady's slipper has two large, simple, oval leaves with parallel veins rising from the base of the flowering stalk, which grows 6 to 12 feet high. Prefers the dry, acid sail of sandy or rocky woods. Also found growing as an ornamental plant.

Part used: Leaves.

Use: (1) Fever—to dry up, place a leaf on the forehead. (2) Headache—bind same leaves tightly around the head with a string.

Euro-American use: Roots used for tonic, to produce perspiration, as nerve stimulant. Tea used for nervous headache.[62]

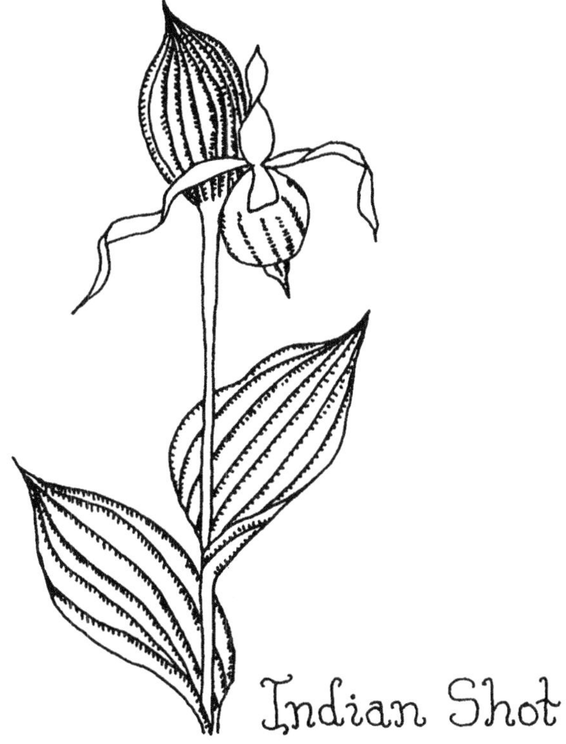

## IRONWEED

(Indian Tobacco)
*Lobelia inflata*

Description: A hairy and branched plant that grows 1 to 3 feet high. Leaves are lance or egg shaped, and toothed. Flowers are small and pale blue; the bases become swollen as the fruits form. Grows in open woods, thickets, and fields, and is indigenous to most parts of the United States.

Part used: Leaves.

Use: Fever—boil small flowers in a tub and bathe in the water.

Euro-American use: Stalk, leaves, and root used for emetic, sedative, relaxant, epilepsy, cramps. Applied externally as ointment.[63]

## IRONWEED, COMMON

*Vernonia augustifolia*

Description: A stiffly erect plant, with coarse stems 3 to 6 feet high. It has long, slender leaves with fine teeth. The plant grows on low ground, along streams and ponds, and in the pinelands of the low country.

Part used: Root.

Use: "The root is used by the negroes in South Carolina as a remedy for the bite of serpents. It is also considered by them to be aphrodisiac."[64]

## JIMSEY

(Jimson Weed)
*Datura stramonium*

Description: A plant that grows 2 to 3 feet high, with large, smooth, deeply lobed leaves. A native of Asia, it is now widely naturalized in fields and roadsides throughout the United States. A potentially poisonous narcotic in large doses, an overdose, which may prove fatal, produces delirium and intense pain.

Part used: Leaves.

Use: To rid the body of worms—boil leaves, strain liquid, and drink.

Official use: The dried leaf was official in the *USP* from 1820 to 1950 and in the *NF* from 1950 to 1965. It is an important source of atropine and widely used in folk medicine.[65]

Other Afro-American use: Colds and respiratory diseases—inhale smoke from burned, dry leaves.[66] Wounds-apply mashed jimson weed or snake oil. Use jimson weed pulp for salve.[67]

Native American use: Narcotic agent for pains. Used in ointment, lotion, and plaster for inflammation and burns. Smoked for shortness of breath and asthma.[68]

Euro-American use: Used in small doses for pain of neuralgia and rheumatism. Leaves smoked for asthma. Used externally for swellings, bruises, wounds, and inflammation.[69]

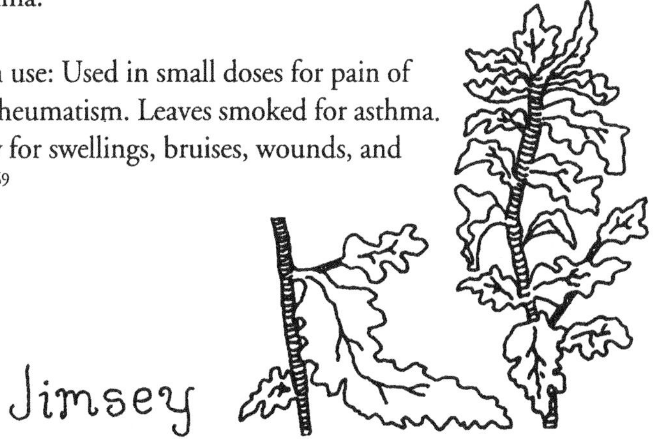

## KIDNEY WEED

(Whorled Milkwort)
*Polygala verticillata*

Description: The very slender stem of the plant is from 6 to 16 inches high. Very narrow leaves are aranged in 3 to 7 whorls. Small purplish, greenish, or whitish flowers appear at the ends of the stalks. It grows in sunny, meadow areas.

Part used: Entire plant.

Use: Diuretic, as the name implies. To flush out the kidneys, drink in the form of tea.

## LAUREL, HAIRY

*Kalmia hirsuta*

Description: An evergreen shrub 6 inches to 2 feet high. Has pink or purple flowers and small, hairy leaves. Grows in moist, sandy pinelands.

Part used: Leaves.

Use: "The leaves are used by negroes, and the poorer white people, as a cure for itch.... A strong decoction in applied warm to the eruptions, which occasions much smarting, and it seldom requires more than one application to effect a cure."[70]

"Elliott states that the negroes of Carolina use the leaves of *Kalmia augustifolia* (sheep laurel) and *Kalmia hirsuta* in a strong wash to cure the itch of men and dogs; it smarts, but cures effectively."[71]

## LIFE EVERLASTING

*Gnaphalium polycephalum*

Description: An herbaceous annual. The leaves are dark green on top and silvery on the bottom. At most, the plant grows 1 to 2 feet high. It bears yellow flowers. The leaves have a pleasant, aromatic smell. Found in Canada and the United States in old fields and on dry, barren lands.

Part used: The entire plant.

Use: Cramps—brew into tea. This tea will also make the menstrual period come more easily. Decongestant—boil with snakeroot, pine tar, and lemon; drink. Foot pain—soak the feet in a bath made of life everlasting and warm water. Fever—combine with rignum and brew into a tea. General well being—drink a tea made from the plant.

Other Afro-American use: To relieve toothache—smoke dried and crumbled life everlasting leaves.[72] To prolong life and for a charm against illness—drink the tea.[73]

Native American use: Life everlasting leaves mixed with lard were applied externally to the swollen glands associated with mumps. Until the coming of the European, however, mumps did not exist among native Americans. The leaves and flowers were also chewed for quinsy.[74]

Euro-American use: For bruises, tumors, fever, influenza, ulcerations of the mouth and throat, pulmonary and bronchial complaints, and bowel disorders.[75]

Life Everlasting

## MINT, AMERICAN WILD

*Mentha arvensis*

Description: A smooth plant with a slender, simple or branched stem 6 inches to 2 feet tall. Leaves are narrow and toothed. Flowers are small. True mints, including the familiar peppermint and spearmint, are members of the genus *Mentha.* Only American wild mint is a native plant; the others were introduced from Europe.

Part used: Leaves.

Use: Stomach pain—drink tea.

Official use: The leaves and tops of horsemint were official in the *USP* from 1820 to 1882. Monarda oil, the principal active constituent, was official during the same period. It was used internally for stomach pain, and to produce perspiration. Peppermint oil is used medicinally as an agent to remove an excess of gases from the stomach and intestines.[76]

Native American use: Wild bergamot—chills, stomach pain, colds. Peppermint—pneumonia. Horsemint—cholera, backache; to induce sweating; chills; ague.[77]

Euro-American use: Mint tea for stomach distress, diarrhea, stomach cramps.[78]

## MISTLETOE

*Phoradendrom flavescens, Pursh.*

Description: An evergreen, yellowish green, shrubby plant that is parasitic in the branches of oaks and broad-leaved trees. Leaves are thick and leathery.

Part used: Leaves.

Use: Rinse for hair.

Euro-American use: Well-known Christmas decoration.

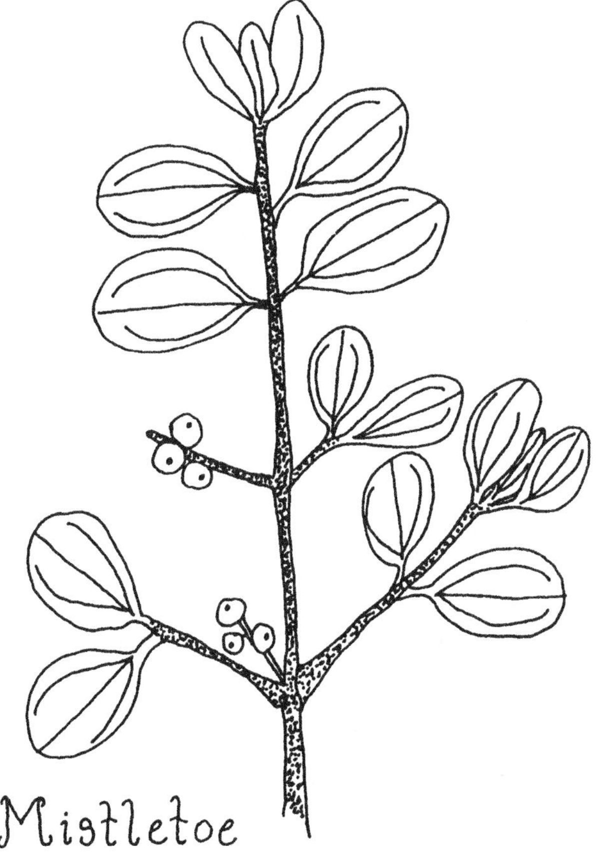

## MOSS, GREEN

*Tillandsia usneoides*
(Spanish Moss)

Description: An epiphytic plant that forms pendant tufts of hair-like, grayish green strands on the trunks and branches of many trees in the southern United States and the West Indies. Also called black moss, long moss, and old man's beard.

Part used: Whole plant.

Use: Invigorating bath—place the green moss in water and bathe as normal. High blood pressure—brew water and moss and drink. Sprains—either wrap around sprains alone or mix with clay and vinegar.

## MUCKLES

That there are at least three kinds of muckles is certain; some informants also identified fourth and fifth types. The three types identified by everyone are the brown muckle, marsh muckle, and white muckle. The fourth and fifth types are the red and yellow muckles.

## MUCKLE, BROWN

(Wax Myrtle or Bayberry)
*Myrica cerifera*

Description: An aromatic evergreen shrub or small tree that grows in wet, sandy pinelands and bogs. The leaves are fragrant when crushed and flowers are yellowish. The bluish white berries are the source of bayberry wax, used for candles. The shrub is found in swampy regions throughout the southeastern states.

Part used: Leaves.

Use: Colds—boil leaves and make tea.

Official use: Wax myrtle bark was official in the *NF* from 1916 to 1936, for use as an astringent and tonic.[79]

Native American use: Leaves and stems for fever and as emetic.[80]

Euro-American use: Wax and root bark—stimulant for weak mucous membranes. Bark—sores, ulcers, jaundice. Wax—ulcerated bowels, stomach. Leaves—vomiting, stomach trouble.[81]
*In South Carolina:* Root—diarrhea, dysentery, uterine hemorrhage, dropsy, gargle for sore throat. Leaves—astringent.[82]

## MUCKLE, MARSH

(Sea Muckle)
*Borrichia frutescens*

Description: A shrub 1 to 2½ feet high that grows in salt marshes along the coast. Young leaves are very leathery and fleshy, older ones are thick, grayish green with short, silky hair on both surfaces. The flower is yellow and daisylike; the fruit is burrlike, small, and dry.

Part used: Leaves.

Use: Colds—(1) boil the leaves, strain, and drink; (2) boil the leaves with pine tar, strain, and drink.

## MUCKLE, RED

Part used: Leaves.

Use: To take off ticks.

## MUCKLE, WHITE

(Groundselbush or Sea Myrtle)
*Baccharis halimifolia*

Description: Resinous, semi-evergreen shrub 3 to 10 feet high. Leaves are coarsely toothed and smooth. Grows in swampy thickets; sandy, open woods; fields; and beaches.

Part used: Leaves.

Use: Colds—boil with pine tar and strain. Whooping cough—boil and mix with boiled fiddler crabs. Strain and drink.

## MUCKLE, YELLOW

Part used: Leaves.

Use: Colds and fever—boil with pine tar and strain before drinking.

## MULLEIN

*Verbascum*

Description: The stem of this plant rises to a maximum height of approximately 7 feet, and has thick, velvety leaves. The stem is crowned with a long, dense spike of yellow leaves. A common pasture "weed," it is partial to recently made clearings, fields, and roadsides. Mullein was introduced to this country from Europe, where it had long been used as a medicinal plant.

Parts used: Leaves and flowers.

Use: For colds, fevers, and swollen limbs—boil the leaves and wrap them around the body.

Official use: Mullein leaves and flowers were listed in the *NF* from 1916 to 1936, classified as demulcents. The leaves were also classified as emollients.[83]

Other Afro-American use: Colds—mullein leaf tea.

*In South Carolina:* Backache—mullein, pokeroot, alum, salt, and jimson weed, mixed.[84] Kidney diseases—mullein "tree" tea, so called because of the plant's height.[85]

Native American use: Asthma, sore throat. Leaves as poultice for pains and swellings, sprains, bruises, wounds, and headaches. Smoked for pulmonary disorders.[86]

Euro-American use: Coughs, catarrh, diarrhea; externally for piles, ulcers, tumors, sores, gout, sore throat. Mixed with other herbs for asthma.[87]

Mullein

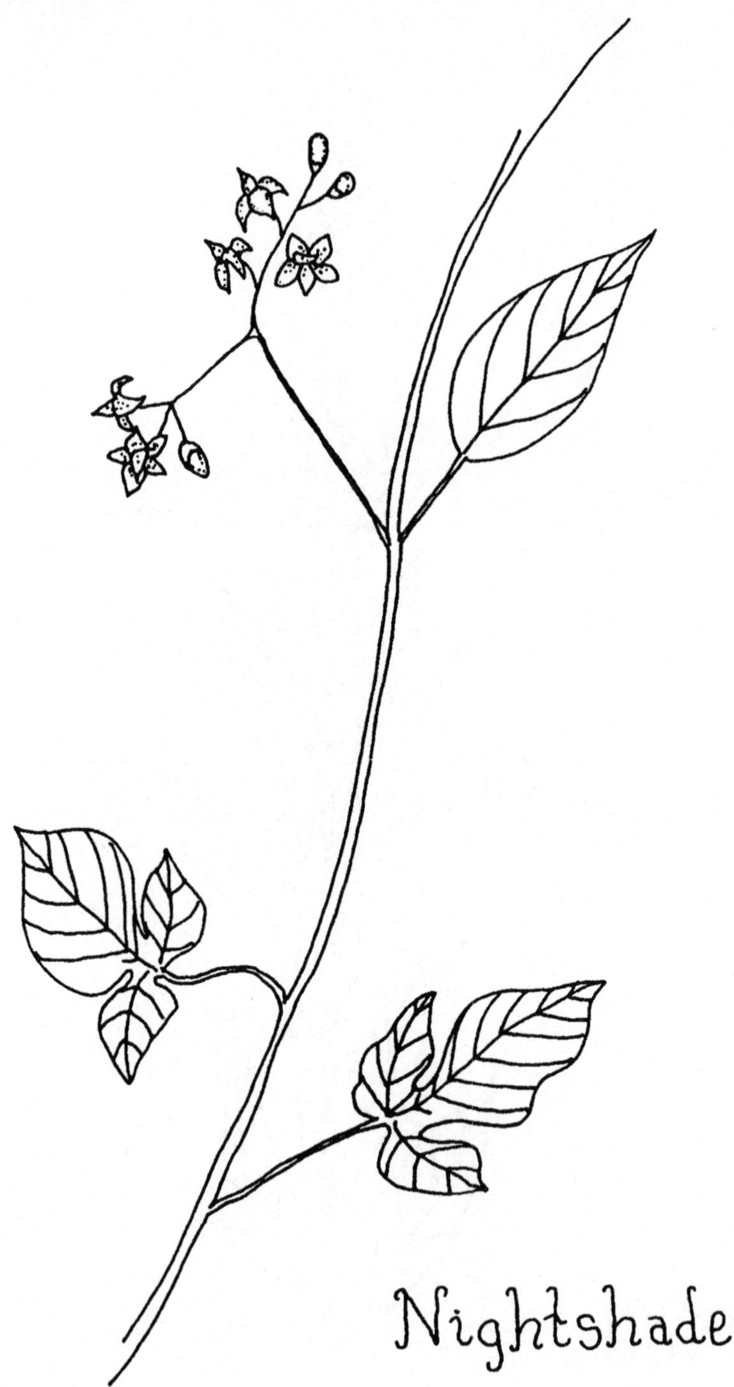
Nightshade

## NIGHTSHADE

*Solanum nigrum*

Description: A bushy herb with a fibrous root and a branching, thornless stem 1 or 2 feet high. Leaves are ovate and smooth, flowers are white or pale violet. The fruit is a berry. Found growing along old walls and fences, and in gardens. This species has been used in medicine, especially for inflammations, from the time of Dioscorides (A.D. 54). Not to be confused with deadly nightshade.[88]

Part used: Root.

Use: Fever—boil the root and drink the tea.

Other Afro-American use:

*In South Carolina:* To promote healing of sores—make a poultice of nightshade leaves. Leave the poultice on for 24 hours.[89]

Native American use: General tonic for tuberculosis, expulsion of worms, sores, insomnia.[90]

Euro-American use: Dropsy, nervous affections, inflammation of mucous membranes, narcotic.[91]

## OAK, RED

(Spanish Oak)
*Quercus falcata, Michx.*

Description: The southern red oak is a medium to large-sized tree, growing 60 to 80 feet high. Prefers dry hills and sandy soil. Tannic acid is obtained from the bark.

Part used: Bark.

Use: Rub for limbs derived from bark. Bark boiled in water is also used for an invigorating bath. "Red oak bark tea is used for backache."[92]

Other Afro-American use: "We have ourselves found the bark of the tree of some service among the negroes, in special cases, where a tonic astringent injection was required, using it in one case of prolapsus uteri, where the organ became chafed and painful from exposure."[93] Tea made from red oak bark taken from the right side of the tree relieves toothache.[94] Menstrual pain—red oak bark tea. Chills and fever—red oak bark tea mixed with turpentine and salt.[95]

Euro-American use: Externally for cancers, ulcers; internally for diarrhea, sore throat, hemorrhages.[96]

*In Georgia:* Malaria—dogwood, cherry bark, and red oak bark tea. For inflammation, make a strong tea of red oak bark and mix with meal and cook to a mush. Make a poultice by spreading on a cloth while hot and place on wound.[97]

## OIL BUSH

(Fever Bush)
*Laurus benzoin*

Description: This shrub ranges in height from 6 to 15 feet, and is found in richly wooded areas. Berries contain a highly aromatic oil.

Part used: Leaves.

Use: Fever, and as a binding for the head. Bathe in the leaves or wrap the body in them.

Euro-American use: "Extensively used in North America in intermittent fever."[98] Oil from berries applied to bruises, rheumatic limbs. For fevers and to produce sweating.[99]

## OKRA

(Gombo)
*Hibiscus esculentus*

Description: Introduced into this country from Africa, okra grows chiefly in the southern United States. It is a tall annual that is widely cultivated for its mucilaginous green pods that are pickled or used as the basis for soups and stews.

Part used: Blossoms.

Use: Sores that don't heal—(1) place the blossoms alone on the sores; or (2) mix the raw blossoms with octagon soap and sugar, and place this mixture on the sore.

Other Afro-American use: "The parched seeds (of okra) afford a tolerable good substitute for coffee; the difference can with difficulty be detected. It is sometimes used for this purpose among the negroes on the plantations in South Carolina."[100]

Euro-American use:
*In Louisiana:* Pounded okra blossoms are mixed with sugar to bring a boil to a head.[101]

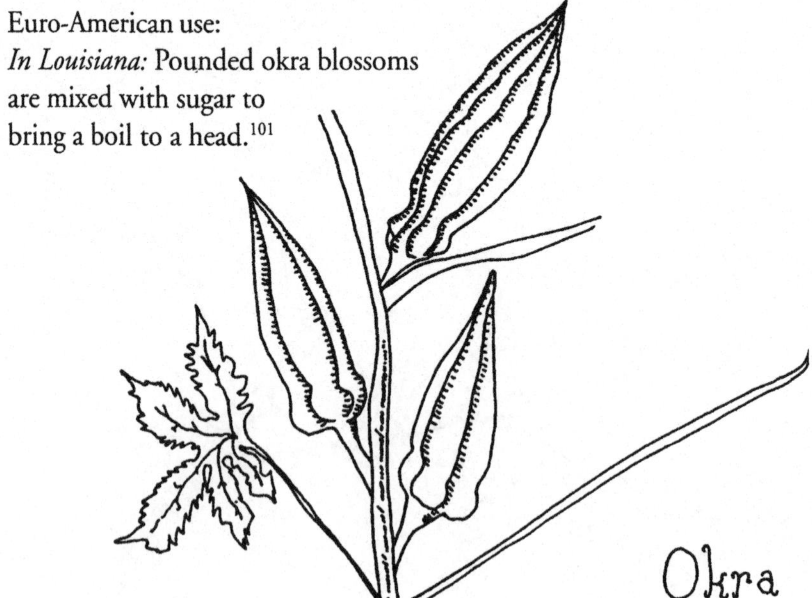

## OLD HAG'S TABLE

(Mushroom)

Description: The name describes a type of fungus rather than a specific species. The mushroom in question may be large or small, but it must be shaped like a stool or table.

Part used: Whole mushroom.

Use: Sores—place inner brown membranes and dust (spores) on sores.

Other Afro-American use: Toodstool—cut off top, dry it; then dampen with camphor or whiskey. Rub this on limbs to cure sprains and rheumatism.[102]

Native American use: Puffballs—to stop bleeding from cuts and wounds.[103]

## ONION, RED

*Allium*

Description: Introduced to this country from Europe, this widely cultivated plant is actually native to Asia. It has slender, hollow, tubular leaves and an edible, rounded bulb made up of close, concentric layers. The bulb has a notably sharp taste and smell. It is widely used as a vegetable.

Part used: Bulb.

Use: For colds in the chest or shortness of breath, eat the onions raw.

Official use: Onions are known to contain a volatile oil carrying bactericidal properties; therefore, they are of value in destroying germs.[104]

Other Afro-American use: "Drink a gill of red onion juice, and a pint of horsemint tea, twice a day for kidney gravel and stones." This remedy was communicated by a slave to a Baptist minister of Virginia, who was cured by it, and afterwards bought the slave and set him free.[105]

*In South Carolina:* A necklace of mashed onions was worn about the neck to prevent diptheria.[106]

Native American use: Colds—onions were chopped and made into a syrup or used as a poultice.[107]

Euro-American use: Roasted union juice for croup.[108]

*In Georgia:* To improve the kidneys, consume large amounts of onions, raw or cooked.[109]

## PINE TAR

*Pinus*

Description: Pines have needle-shaped leaves arranged in 2 to 5 bundles. These needles persist on the branches for 2, 3, or more years. Flowers develop into the familiar woody-scaled cones. Some obtain the tar by inserting a stick into the trunk of the pine tree. Others obtain it by boiling the needles.

Part used: The sap from pine trees.

Use: Colds—boil with marsh muckle and drink the tea. Decongestant—boil with snakeroot, life everlasting, and lemon: drink tea. Fevers—boil with holly bush: drink tea. Stomach ache—boil with pokeroot and epsom salts: drink tea. Whooping cough—boil alone and drink.

Official use: From 1820 to 1950, pine tar was listed in the *USP* as an antibacterial, an expectorant, and a parasiticide.[110] From 1950 on it was so listed in the *NF*.

Other Afro-American use:

*In South Carolina:* Spring tonic.[111]

Native American use: Inflammation, swellings, burns, tetter, itch, sore throat, colds, and consumption.[112]

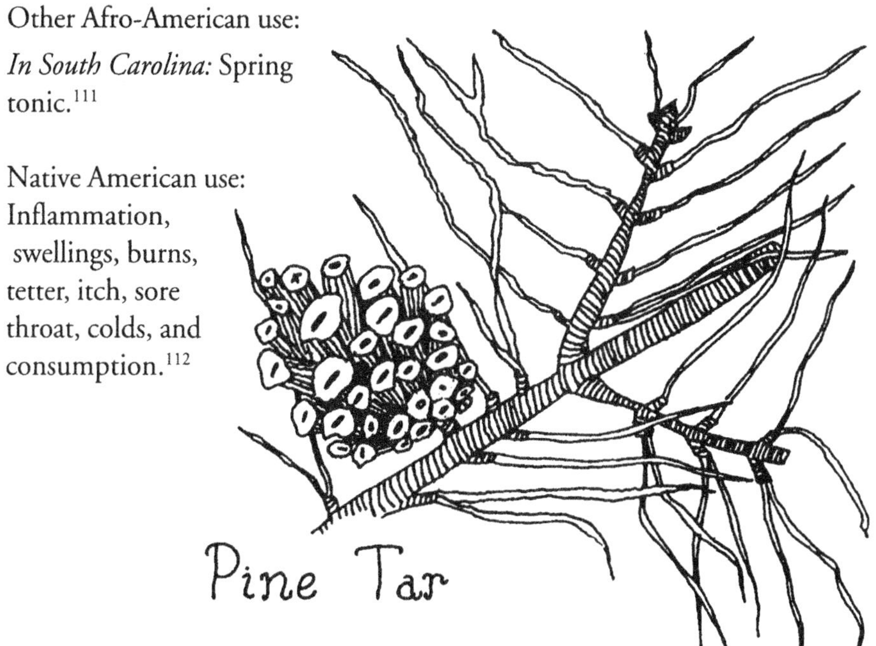

## POKEROOT

*Phytolacca decandra*

Description: The plant stem is annual, ranging from 5 to 9 feet high. Flowers are small and greenish white, the berries round and dark purple, the perennial root fleshy and fibrous. Pokeroot is indigenous to the United States. It grows in dry fields, on hillsides, and on roadsides. The female plant is the one used for medicinal purposes. It is distinguished from the male by its larger root and its berries. Ink can be made from the berries.

Parts used: Leaves and root.

Use: Confinement colds—boil the root and drink the tea. General pain—boil the root, drink the tea. Stomach pain-combine the leaves with pine tar and epsum salts, boil and drink.

Official use: Dried pokeroot was official in the *USP* from 1820 to 1916 and in the *NF* from 1916 to 1947.[113]

Other Afro-American use: To lose weight—place some pokeroot in whiskey and drink.[114] Scrofula—get some roots from the chinaberry tree and some pokeroot. Boil them together, adding a piece of bluestone, and strain carefully. Salve the sores with this mixture and then anoint them with a feather dipped into pure hog lard. This brings the sore to a head; press out the core and you are cured.[115] Laxative—pokeberry juice.[116]

Native American use: Pokeberry—as an emetic and as a tea to cure rheumatism; the powdered root—a poultice for fever.[117]

Euro-American use: Pokeweed berries were used to relieve rheumatism; the root was used as an emetic and to cure syphilis; and the juice of the old plant was used to relieve ulcers, itch, inflammations of the skin, and hemorrhoids.[118]

## RIGNUM

Parts used: Leaves or whole plant.

Use: Fevers—mix with life everlasting, boil, strain, and drink tea. General tonic—boil, strain, and drink tea.

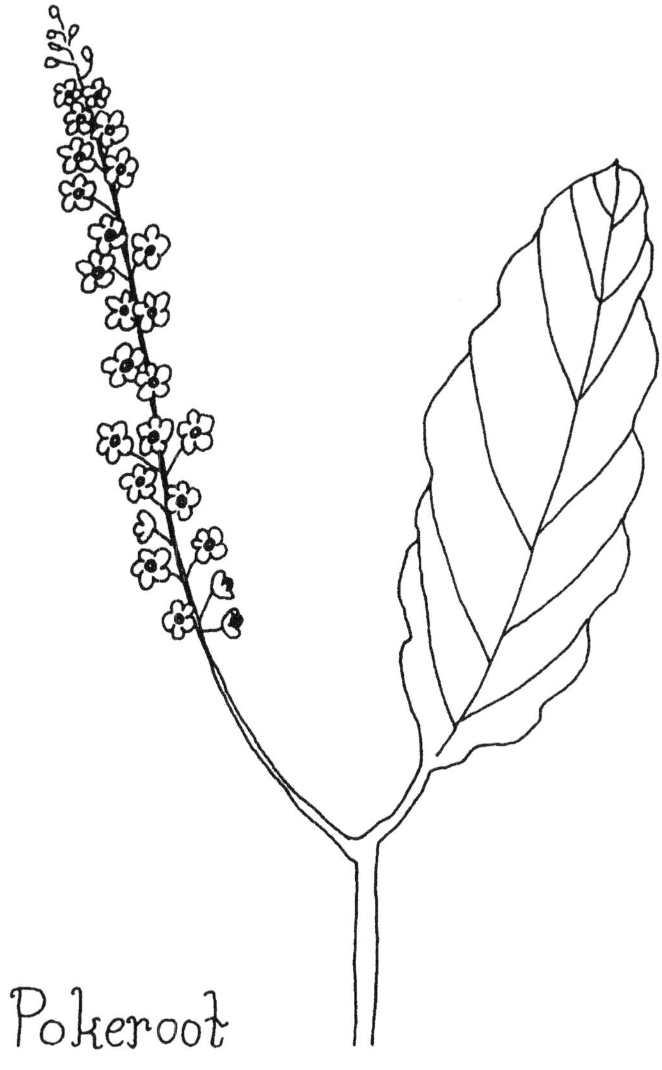

## ST. JOHN'S
*Hypericum*

Description: A small-leaved perennial that grows to a foot or more in height. The flowers are small and yellow. St. John's was introduced to the United States from Europe, where it had been used in medicine since ancient times. It grows in meadows and wooded areas. At one time, St. John's was very common in the Sea Islands, but it is becoming increasingly difficult to find.

Part used: Entire plant.

Use: Sores—bathe in a solution made of warm water and St. John's.

Native American use: Respiratory ailments.[119]

European use: Diuretic; to kill internal worms. It was gathered in Europe on St. John's Day for "mania" and hysteria.

Euro-American use: Diuretic, croup, to clear respiratory obstructions.[120]

## SASSAFRAS

*Laurus sassafras*

Description: Sassafras is a small tree that ranges from 10 to 40 feet in height. The bark is rough and grayish, and the leaves are bright green. Sassafras is indigenous to the United States, and is most commonly found in wooded areas from eastern Canada to Florida. Sassafras root should be dug in the fall to gain the maximum benefit from it.

Part used: Root bark.

Use: Body strength—drink tea made from the roots. General health—same as above. Backache—bathe in sassafras root tea.[121]

Official use: Dried sassafras root bark was official in the *USP* from 1820 to 1926, and in the *NF* from 1926 to 1965.[122]

Other Afro-American use: If a patient is coming down with measles, sassafras tea will bring out the spots and hasten recovery. To purify the blood—drink red sassafras tea.[123]

*In South Carolina:* Tea from "white" sassafras root will cure blindness.[124] Sassafras tea is also used as a spring tonic.[125]

Native American use: Leaves—for poultices. Pith—for eye wash. Roots—to promote the eruption of rash in measles and in measles and scarlet fever; to relieve coughing, pain in the bladder, and low fevers.[126]

Euro-American use: Sassafras became one of the most important export articles early in the history of the United States, the bulk of the shipment going to England for treatment of colic, venereal disease, and general pain. Sassafras was an important domestic tonic for treating rheumatism and high blood pressure, and as a spring renovator of the blood. It was also combined with mare's milk for an eye wash.[127]

## SEDGE

*Cyperus articulatus*

Description: Sedges are grasslike plants that usually grow in moist or wet places.

Use: "In Guinea, this is considered one of their remedies for worms."[128] Unfortunately Porcher does not indicate its specific medical use in South Carolina.

## SENNA, AMERICAN

*Cassia marilandica*

Description: A perennial herb that grows 4 to 6 feet high, with narrow, long leaflets, several of which share one stem. The flowers are bright yellow and the fruit is a legume. The leaves are gathered while the plant is in bloom for best medicinal value.

Part used: Leaves.

Use: "Negroes apply [American senna] leaves smeared with grease as a dressing for sores."[129]

Euro-American use: American senna was an important herbal cathartic.[130]

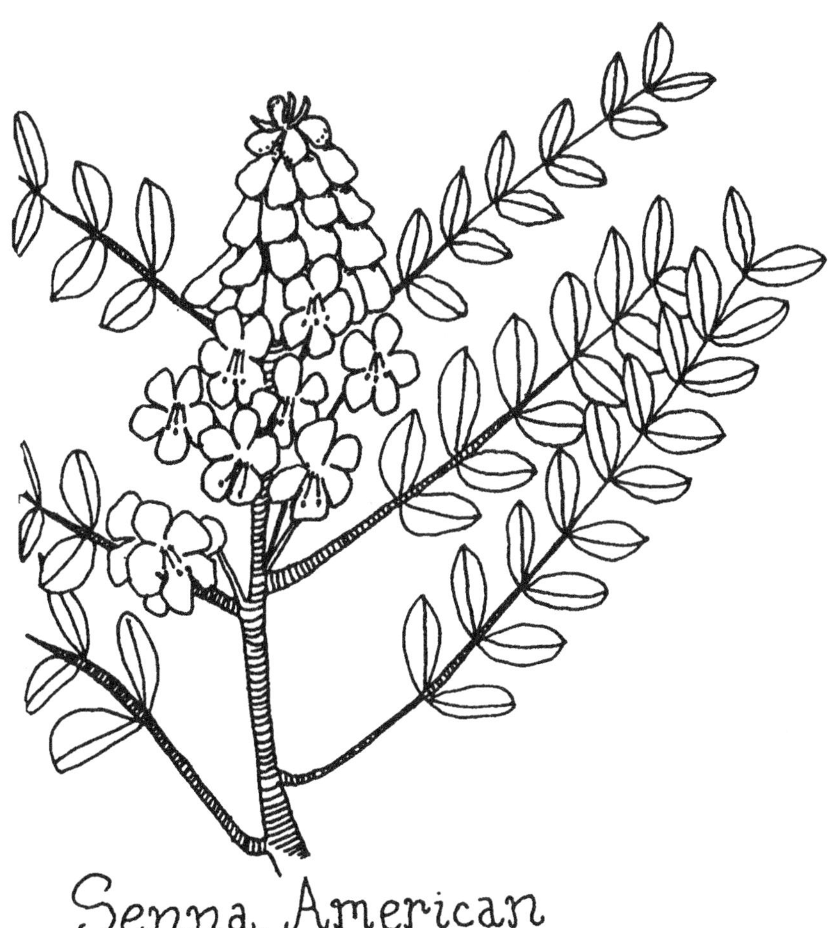

Senna, American

## SNAKEROOT

The term snakeroot has been applied to at least ten different plants. Three are listed here.

## SNAKEROOT, BUTTON

*Eryngium yuccifolium*

Description: An indigenous plant that grows in swamps and low, wet lands from Virginia to Texas. The stem is 1 to 5 feet high, the root is a tuber, and the leaves are 1 to 2 feet long, tapering to a point. Flowers are white or pale; the plant blossoms in the early fall.

Part used: Root.

Use: Because snakeroot is very bitter, it is best to take it as a tea mixed with whiskey. To cut mucus, mix snakeroot with pine tar, life everlasting, and lemon. It may also be taken for colds and to rid the body of worms.

Native American use: As a diuretic; for neuralgia, kidney trouble, snakebite, rheumatism, and as a blood purifier.[131]

Euro-American use: Emetic and diuretic for pleurisy, colds, inflammation of mucous membranes.[132]

## SNAKEROOT, SAMPSON'S

*Gentiana ochroleuca*

Description: A short-stemmed plant 1 to 2 inches high, with straw-colored flowers. The leaves are 2 to 4 inches long.

Parts used: The root, often the leaves.

Use: See button snakeroot.

Other Afro-American use: Indigestion—Sampson's snakeroot tea. Universal liniment—Sampson's snakeroot, red coonroot, and camphor or whiskey.[133]

Native American use: To stop pains in the stomach or to cure backache, brew into a hot or cold infusion, or chew the roots.

Euro-American use: Respiratory problems, dyspepsia, dysentery, snake-bite, pneumonia, to "invigorate the stomach."[134]

## SNAKEROOT, WHITE

Description: The plant has a smooth, many-branched stem with pairs of large, egg-shaped leaves 3 to 6 inches long. It grows in woods, thickets, and clearings.

Part used: Root.

Use: See button snakeroot.

Afro-American use: "Much use is made of this plant [snakeroot in general] among the negroes in this state, particularly in the low stages of pneumonia, to which they are particularly liable."[135]

Euro-American use: Tonic, diuretic, fever. Phthisic in children—snakeroot mixed with licorice stick, parsley root, and honey.[136]

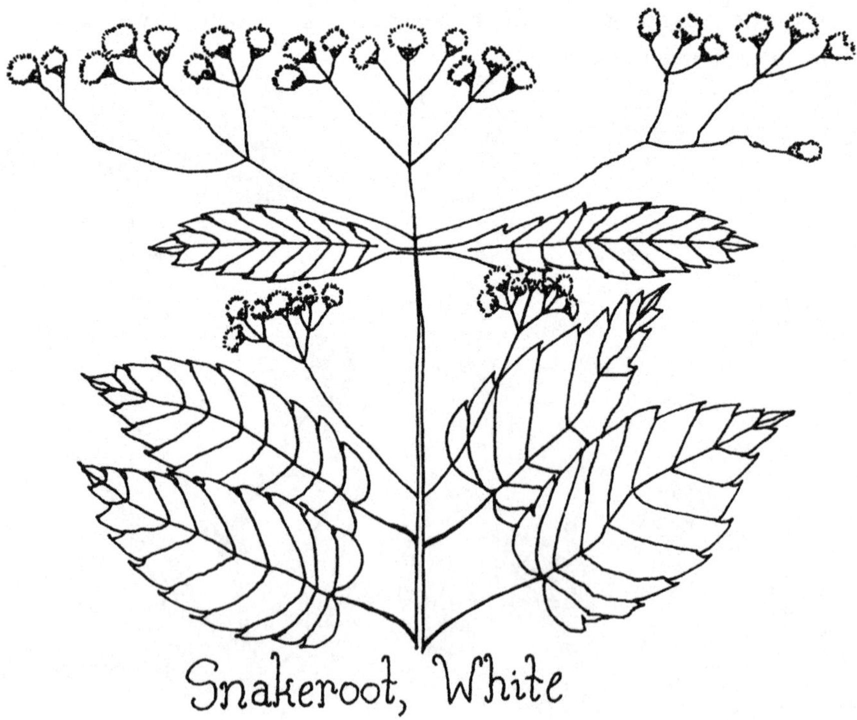

## SPEEDWELL

*Veronica officinalis*

Description: Speedwell creeps over the ground sending up branches 3 to 18 inches high. It is hairy all over. The flowers are pale blue. Although this plant was not described to me under this name, it is probably still used on the Sea Islands. It also grows in West Africa.

Parts used: Leaves and flowering tops.

Use: "This is tonic and pectoral; used in asthmas and coughs; the infusion of the leaves is employed, on the west coast of Africa, as a drink in gravelly complaints. It contains tannin."[137]

Official use: Referred to in the *USP* as a diaphoretic, diuretic, and expectorant.[138]

## SUTRAS

Description: A large bush with large leaves and purple berries. Sutras generally grows in sandy fields.

Part used: Leaves.

Use: Loss of sight—brew the leaves and drop the liquid into the eyes. Sores that don't heal—remove the berries and brew the leaves. Place the liquid on the sores.

## SWAMP GRASS

(Swamp Root or Virginia Snakeroot)
*Aristolochia serpentaria*

Description: An erect plant with a slender, wavy stem 6 to 18 inches tall. The thin, heart-shaped leaves have pointed tips. The plant grows in thick woodlands.

Part used: Leaves.

Use: For relief of sprains—make a poultice from the leaves and apply.

Native American use: Snakebite—chew the root and apply this poultice to the snakebite.[139]

Euro-American use: The plant called swamp grass is also known as Virginia snakeroot. As such, it was the first native American snakebite remedy and accepted in the *USP*. It was also employed for tonic and stimulant purposes.[140] Mixed with sage tea, the root was used for fever and ague. Other applications were: to cure smallpox and pneumonia, and as a poultice for open wounds.[141]

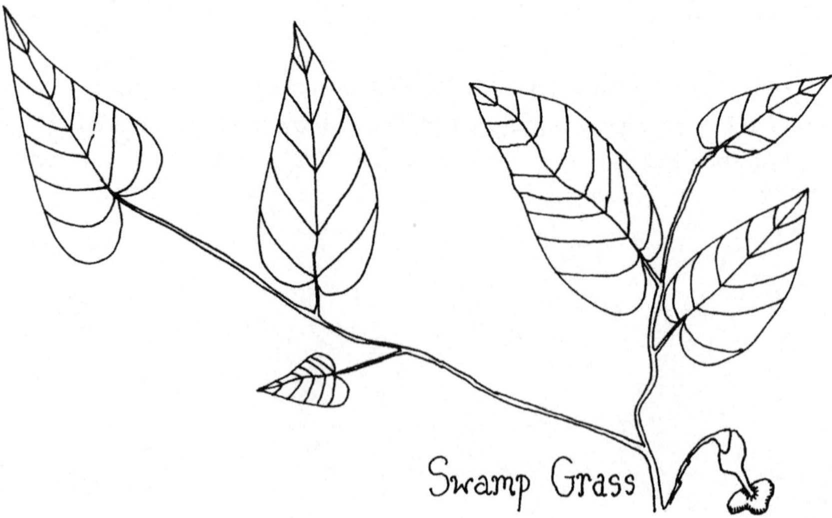

## TADAWAS

*Aster*

Description: A member of the aster family. Asters bloom chiefly in the late summer and fall. The flowers are white, lavender, blue, pink, or purple. There are more than 75 species of aster in eastern North America; consequently, it is not easy to identify individual species.

Part used: Leaves.

Use: Fevers—drink tea made from leaves.

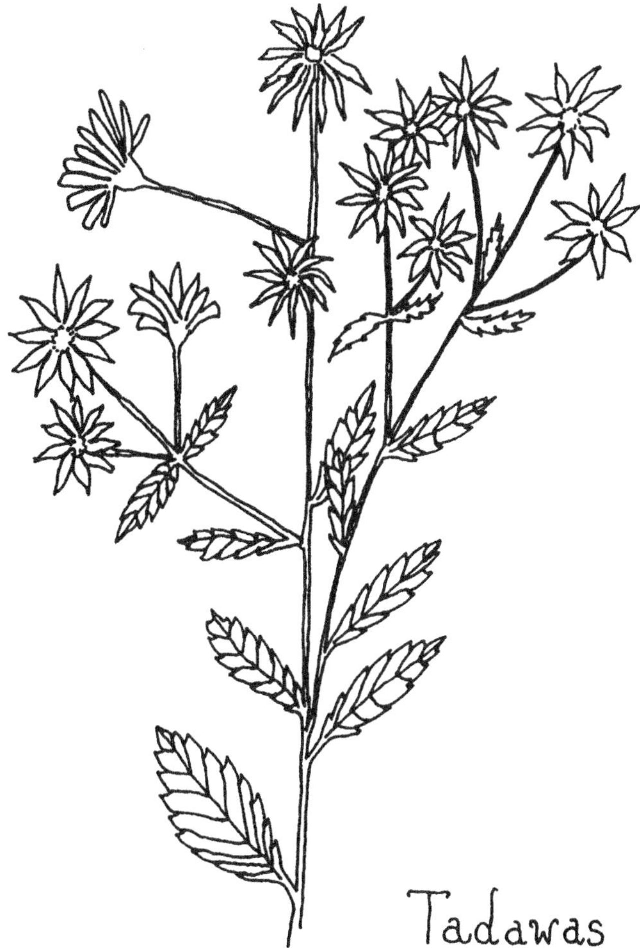

## WHITEROOT

*Lyonia mariana*

Description: A shrub growing to 4 feet, with slender, upright branches. It grows in peaty or sandy open woods. The leaves are bright green and smooth above, paler and bearing minute black dots on the underside. The foliage is poison to calves and lambs if eaten. The root is about 3 inches wide and quite long.

Part used: Root.

Use: For bed, body, and confinement colds; for fevers; and to have children—drink tea made from the root.

# *Plant Cures Used in the Sea Islands*

Aphrodisiac
- common ironweed
- cotton root
- horsenettle, alone or with blackroot, black pepper, bloodroot

Arthritis
- cherry bark

Asthma
- speedwell

Backache
- red oak bark
- sassafras root

Bath, invigorating
- green moss
- red oak bark

Blood pressure, high
- galax
- green moss

Breath, shortness of
- galax
- red onions

Burns
- cow dung, spittle

Colds, general
- brown muckle
- button snakeroot
- boneset
- marsh muckle, alone or with pine tar
- mullein
- pine tar, alone or with herbs
- sweet gum

(Colds, general)
- yellow muckle, pine tar

Colds, bed
- white root

Colds, body
- black root
- whiteroot

Colds, chest
- red onions

Colds, confinement
- blackroot
- pokeroot
- whiteroot

Colic
- American aloe

Conception, for
- whiteroot

Coughs
- speedwell

Cramps
- life everlasting

Cuts
- spider webs, turpentine

Decongestant
- life everlasting, snakeroot, pine tar, lemon

Diaphoretic
- boneset

Diuretic
- Jerusalem artichoke
- kidney weed

Dropsy
- Jerusalem artichoke

Fever
- bitter apple
- boneset
- holly, pine tar
- Indian shot
- ironweed
- life everlasting, rignum
- mullein
- nightshade
- oil bush
- tadawas
- whiteroot
- yellow muckle, pine tar

Foot pain
- life everlasting

Gravelly voice
- speedwell

Griping
- blackberry

Hair rinse
- mistletoe

Headaches
- Indian shot (bind head)
- soda, hot water
- squeeze the head
- wear a string tied around head knotted to draw the pain

Hemorrhage
- cob webs and soot (while giving birth)

Itch
- hairy laurel

Jaundice
- Jerusalem artichoke

Kidneys
- kidney weed

Menstruation
- life everlasting

Pain, general
- comfrey
- poke root

Poultices
- clay and green moss, alone and together
- swamp grass

Pregnancy, colds during
- blackroot
- pokeroot
- whiteroot

Respiration
- speedwell

Rheumatism
- Angelica tree

Sight, loss of
- sutras

Snakebite
- American aloe
- Angelica tree
- common ironweed

Sores
- American senna
- elderberry
- gum tree
- okra blossoms, alone or with octagon soap, sugar
- old hag's table
- St. John's
- sutras

Sprains
- blue clay
- camphor, green alcohol
- clay, alone, with green moss, and with vinegar
- red clay
- swamp grass

Stimulants
- Angelica tree
- cotton root

Stings
- fennel

Stomach pain
- American wild mint
- blackberry root
- pine tar, pokeroot, epsom salts
- sweet gum

Strength
- sassafras

Swollen limbs
- mullein

Ticks
- red muckle

Tonics
- boneset
- Jerusalem artichoke
- life everlasting
- rignum
- sassafras
- speedwell

Typhoid pneumonia
- boneset

Whooping cough
- pine tar
- white muckle, fiddler crabs

Worms
- ayshaberry
- button snakeroot
- jimsey
- Sampson's snakeroot
- white snakeroot

# Notes

[1]Francis P. Porcher, "Report on the Indigenous Medical Plants of South Carolina," Transactions of the American Medical Association 2 (1849): 833.

[2]Joseph E. Meyer, *The Herbalist* (Hammond, Ind.: Hammond Book Co., (1934), p. 16.

[3]Porcher, "Medical Plants," p. 703.

[4]Ibid.

[5]Porcher, "Medical Plants," pp. 798-99.

[6]Dr. Newbell Niles Puckett, Folk Beliefs of the Southern Negro (Montclair, N.J.: Patterson Smith, 1968), p. 364.

[7]Clarence Meyer. *American Folk Medicine* (New York: Thomas Y. Crowell Co., 1973), p. 132.

[8]Meyer, *The Herbalist,* p. 40

[9]Dr. Ronald G. Killion and Dr. Charles T. Walker, *A Treasury of Georgia Folklore* (Atlanta, Cherokee Publishing Co., 1972), p. 98.

[10]Meyer, *The Herbalist,* p. 64.

[11]Michael A. Weiner, Earth Medicine-Earth Foods: Plant Remedies, Drugs, and Natural Foods of the North American Indians (New York: Macmillan, 1972), p.48; and Virgil J. Vogel, *American Indian Medicine* (Norman: University of Oklahoma Press, 1970), p. 282.

[12]Personal communication from E.E. Mitchell.

[13]Weiner, *Earth Medicine,* p. 48; Vogel, *American Indian Medicine,* p. 282; and Ensign Lloyd G. Carr and Carlos Westey, "Surviving Folktales and Herbal Lore Among the Shinnecock Indians of Long Island," *Journal of American Folklore 58* (April-June 1945): 119.

[14]Vogel, *American Indian Medicine.* p. 282; *Every Man His Own Doctor! A Medical Handbook* (Hinsdale, N.H.: Hunter and Co., 1870), p. 63.

[15]Killion and Walker, *Georgia Folklore,* p. 100.

[16]Lyle Saxon, Edward Dreyer, Robert Tallant, *Gumbo Ya-Ya* (Louisiana Writer's Project 1945. New York: Johnson Reprint Corp., 1969), p. 533.

[17]Porcher, "Medical Plants," p. 794.

[18]Dr. O. Phelps Brown, *The Complete Herbalist, or, The People Their Own Physicians, by the Use of Nature's Remedies, Describing the Great Curative Properties Found in the Herbal Kingdom* (Jersey City, NJ.: published by the author, 1874), p. 143.

[19]Puckett, *Folk Beliefs,* p. 331.

[20]Killion and Walker, *Georgia Folklore,* p.70.

[21]Brown, *The Complete Herbalist,* p. 143.

[22]Porcher, "Medical Plants," p. 791.

[23]Ibid.; and Meyer, *The Herbalist,* p. 48.

[24]Weiner, *Earth Medicine.* pp. 42, 119; and Vogel, *American Indian Medicine,* p. 388.

[25]Puckett, *Folk Beliefs,* p. 386.

[26]Personal communication from E. E. Mitchell.

[27]Vogel, *American Indian Medicine,* p. 388; Weiner, *Earth Medicine,* p. 42; and Carr and Westey, "Surviving Folktales," p. 118.

[28]Weiner, *Earth Medicine,* p. 42; and Meyer, *American Folk Medicine,* pp. 36, 40.
[29]Killion and Walker, *Georgia Folklore,* p. 112.
[30]Puckett, *Folk Beliefs,* p. 360.
[31]Ibid., p.378; and Verta Grosvenor, *Vibration Cooking or the Travel Notes of a Geechee Girl* (New York: Doubleday and Co., 1970), p. 136.
[32]Meyer, *American Folk Medicine,* pp. 232, 274.
[33]Killion and Walker, *Georgia Folklore,* p. 95.
[34]*His Own Doctor.!* p.71; and Brown, *The Complete Herbalist,* p. 73.
[35]Vogel, *American Indian Medicine,* p. 295; and Weiner, *Earth Medicine,* p. 9.
[36]*Weiner, Earth Medicine,* p. 9; and *John U. Lloyd, History of the Vegetable Drugs of the Pharmacopeia of the United States* (Cincinnati: J. V. and C. G. Lloyd, 1911), pp. 43-44.
[37]Vogel, *American Indian Medicine,* p.295; and Weiner, *Earth Medicine,* p. 9.
[38]*His Own Doctor!* p. 72; Brown, *The Complete Herbalist,* p. 95; and Porcher, "Medical Plants," p. 721.
[39]Vogel, *American Indian Medicine,* p. 301; and Weiner, *Earth Medicine,* p. 38.
[40]Puckett, *Folk Beliefs,* p. 378.
[41]Ibid., p. 388.
[42]Vogel, *American Indian Medicine,* p. 301; Weiner, *Earth Medicine,* p. 38.
[43]Dr. Charles F. Millspaugh, *American Medicinal Plants. An Illustrated and Descriptive Guide to the American Plants Used as Homeopathic Remedies* (New York and Philadelphia: Boeriche and Tafel, 1887), plant no. 75; *His Own Doctor!* p. 76; Brown, *The Complete Herbalist,* p.84; and Vogel, *American Indian Medicine,* p.301.
[44]Killion and Walker, *Georgia Folklore,* p. 109.
[45]Puckett, *Folk Beliefs,* p. 331.
[46]Ibid., p. 364.
[47]Grosvenor, *Vibration Cooking,* p. 143.
[48]*His Own Doctor!* p.76; and Porcher, "Medical Plants," p. 700.
[49]Killion and Walker, *Georgia Folklore,* p. 98.
[50]Vogel, *American Indian Medicine,* p. 306.
[51]Ibid.; and Weiner, *Earth Medicine,* p. 74.
[52]Vogel, *American Indian Medicine,* p. 306; and Weiner, *Earth Medicine,* p. 74.
[53]Weiner, *Earth Medicine,* p. 13.
[54]Puckett, *Folk Beliefs,* p. 369.
[55]Weiner, *Earth Medicine,* p. 13.
[56]Brown, *The Complete Herbalist,* p. 158, and *His Own Doctor!* p. 99.
[57]Killion and Walker, *Georgia Folklore,* p. 97.
[58]Puckett, *Folk Beliefs,* p. 387.
[59]Porcher, "Medical Plants," p. 782.
[60]Porcher, "Medical Plants," p. 818.
[61]*His Own Doctor!* p. 88.
[62]Meyer, *The Herbalist,* p. 178.
[63]Brown, *The Complete Herbalist,* p. 116.
[64]Porcher, "Medical Plants," p. 790.
[65]Vogel, *American Indian Medicine,* p. 326.

[66]Puckett, *Folk Beliefs*, p. 369.

[67]Ibid., p. 377.

[68]Vogel, *American Indian Medicine*, p. 326.

[69]Brown, *The Complete Herbalist*. p. 108; and *His Own Doctor!* p. 98.

[70]Porcher, "Medical Plants," p. 779.

[71]Meyer, *American Folk Medicine*, p. 148.

[72]Puckett, *Folk Beliefs*, p. 372.

[73]Lewis de Claremont, *Legends of Incense, Herb Oil and Magic*, 2d ed., rev. (Dallas: Dorene Publishing Co., 1966), p. 84.

[74]Weiner, *Earth Medicine*, p. 96.

[75]Millspaugh, *American Medicinal Plants*, plant no. 89; *His Own Doctor!* p. 102; Brown, *The Complete Herbalist*, p.130; and Porcher, "Medical Plants," p. 797.

[76]Weiner, *Earth Medicine*, p. 95; and Vogel, *American Indian Medicine*, p. 337.

[77]Ibid.

[78]Meyer, *American Folk Medicine*, pp. 91, 236.

[79]Vogel, *American Indian Medicine*, p. 279.

[80]Ibid.; and Weiner, *Earth Medicine*, p. 57.

[81]Brickell, *The Natural History of North Carolina, with an Account of the Trade, Manners and Customs of the Christian and Indian Inhabitants* (Dublin, 1737), cited in Vogel, *American Indian Medicine, p.* 279; and Millspaugh, *American Medicinal Plants*, plant no. 160.

[82]Porcher, "Medical Plants," pp. 759-60.

[83]Vogel, *American Indian Medicine*, p. 341.

[84]Puckett, *Folk Beliefs*, pp. 363, 369.

[85]William Dosite Postell, *The Health of Slaves on Southern Plantations* (Baton Rouge: Louisiana State University Press, 1951), p. 109.

[86]Vogel, *American Indian Medicine*, p. 341; and Carr and Westey, "Surviving Folktales." p. 118.

[87]*His Own Doctor!* p. 88; Brown, *The Complete Herbalist*, p. 125; and Porcher, *Medical Plants*, p. 813.

[88]Weiner, *Earth Medicine*, p. 78.

[89]Grosvenor, *Vibration Cooking*, p. 135.

[90]Vogel, *American Indian Medicine*. p.342; and Weiner, Earth Medicine, p. 78.

[91]Millspaugh, *American Medicinal Plants*, plant no. 125.

[92]Elsie Clews Parsons, "Folklore of the Sea Islands, South Carolina," *Memoirs of the American Folklore Society* 16(1923): 212.

[93]Porcher, "Medical Plants," p. 752.

[94]Puckett, *Folk Beliefs*. p. 372.

[95]Ibid., pp. 364, 386.

[96]Brown, *The Complete Herbalist*, p. 129.

[97]Killion and Walker, *Georgia Folklore*, pp. 103, 104.

[98]Porcher, "Medical Plants," p. 765.

[99]Millspaugh, *American Medicinal Plants*, plant no. 145.

[100]Porcher, "Medical Plants," p. 721.

[101]Saxon, Dreyer, Tallant, *Gumbo Ya-Ya*, p. 526.
[102]Puckett, *Folk Beliefs*, p. 246.
[103]Carr and Westey, "Surviving Folktales," p. 121; and Weiner, *Earth Medicine*, p. 143.
[104]T. H. Lovell, "Bactericidal Effect of Onion Vapors," *Food Research* 2 (1937): 435, cited in Carr and Westey, "Surviving Folktales," p. 120.
[105]Meyer, *American Folk Medicine*, p. 161.
[106]H. C. Davis, "Negro Folklore in South Carolina," *Journal of American Folklore* 27 (July-September 1914): 246.
[107]Carr and Westey, "Surviving Folktales," p. 120; and Vogel, *American Indian Medicine*, p. 306.
[108]Vogel, *American Indian Medicine*. p. 306.
[109]Killion and Walker, *Georgia Folklore*. p. 104.
[110]Vogel, *American Indian Medicine*, p. 346.
[111]Grosvenor, *Vibration Cooking*, p. 143.
[112]Vogel, *American Indian Medicine*, p. 346.
[113]Vogel, *American Indian Medicine*, p. 350; and Weiner, *Earth Medicine*, p. 113.
[114]Personal correspondence from E. E. Mitchell.
[115]Puckett, *Folk Beliefs*, p. 384.
[116]Ibid., p. 391.
[117]Vogel, *American Indian Medicine*, p. 350; Millspaugh, *American Medicinal Plants*, plant no.139; and Weiner, *Earth Medicine*, p. 113.
[118]Millspaugh, *American Medicinal Plants*, plant no.139; *His Own Doctor!* p. 91; Brown, *The Complete Herbalist*, p. 137; and Porcher, "Medical Plants," p. 770.
[119]Peter Smith of the Miami Country, *The Indian Doctor's Dispensatory, Being Father Smith's Advice Respecting Diseases and Their Cure* (Cincinnati: Browne and Looker, 1812), reprinted in Bulletin of the Lloyd Library of Botany, Pharmacy and Materia Medica, plant no. 22.
[120]Millspaugh, *American Medicinal Plants*, plant no. 30; and Weiner, *Earth Medicine*, p. 112.
[121]Puckett, *Folk Beliefs*, p. 363.
[122]Vogel, *American Indian Medicine*, p. 361; and Weiner, *Folk Medicine*, p. 86.
[123]Puckett, *Folk Beliefs*, p. 390.
[124]Davis, "Negro Folklore," p. 246.
[125]Grosvenor, *Vibration Cooking*, p. 143.
[126]Vogel, *American Indian Medicine*, p. 361; and Weiner, *Earth Medicine*, p. 86.
[127]Weiner, *Earth Medicine*, p. 86; Brown, *The Complete Herbalist*, p. 150; Porcher, "Medical Plants," p. 764; and Meyer, *American Folk Medicine*, p. 110.
[128]Porcher, "Medical Plants," p. 850.
[129]Porcher, "Medical Plants," p. 744.
[130]Brown, *The Complete Herbalist*, p. 21.
[131]Vogel, *American Indian Medicine*, pp. 368-74.
[132]Porcher, "Medical Plants," p. 698; and Meyer, *The Herbalist*, p. 264.
[133]Vogel, *American Indian Medicine*, p. 307.
[134]Porcher, "Medical Plants," p. 823; and Brown, *The Complete Herbalist*, p. 103.

[135]Porcher, "Medical Plants," p. 766.

[136]Ibid.; and Meyer, *American Folk Medicine*, p. 31.

[137]Porcher, "Medical Plants," p. 815.

[138]Ibid.

[139]Weiner, *Earth Medicine*, p. 126.

[140]Ibid.

[141]Millspaugh, *American Medicinal Plants*, plant no. 138, and Smith, *Indian Doctor's Dispensatory*, plant no. 39.

# Works Cited

## General

Bedenbaugh, J. W. "Note." *Southern Workman* 23 (December 1894): 209-10.

Bennett, John. *The Doctor to the Dead; Grotesque Legends and Folk Tales of Old Charleston.* Columbia: University of South Carolina Press, 1995.

Botkin, B. A., ed. *Lay My Burden Down: A Folk History of Slavery.* Chicago: University of Chicago Press, 1945.

Bowker, Pierpoint E. *The Indian Vegetable Family Instructor.* Boston: published by the author, 1836.

Brown, Dr. O. Phelps. *The Complete Herbalist, or, The People Their Own Physicians, by the use of Nature's Remedies, Describing the Great Curative Properties Found in the Herbal Kingdom.* Jersey City, N.J.: published by the author, 1874.

Byrd, William. *The Secret Diary of William Byrd of Westover, 1709-1712.* Edited by Louis B. Wright and Marion Tinling. Richmond, Va.: The Dietz Press, 1941.

Carawan, Guy and Candie. *Ain't You Got a Right to the Tree of Life?* New York: Simon and Schuster, 1966.

Carr, Ensign Lloyd G., and Westey, Carlos. "Surviving Folktales and Herbal Lore Among the Shinnecock Indians of Long Island." *Journal of American Folklore* 58 (April-June 1945): 113-23.

Crum, Mason. *Gullah Negro Life in the Carolina Sea Islands.* Durham, N.C.: Duke University Press, 1940.

Davis, H. C. "Negro Folklore in South Carolina." *Journal of American Folklore* 27 (July-September 1914): 241-54.

de Claremont, Lewis. *Legends of Incense, Herb Oil and Magic.* 2d ed., rev. Dallas: Dorene Publishing Co., 1966.

*Drums and Shadows; Survival Studies Among the Georgia Coastal Negroes.* Georgia Writers' Project, Work Projects Administration. Garden City: Anchor Books, 1972.

*Every Man His Own Doctor! A Medical Handbook.* Hinsdale, N.H.: Hunter and Co., 1870.

Georgia Writers' Project. *Drums and Shadows.* New York: Doubleday Anchor, 1972.

Gonzales, Ambrose E. *The Black Border.* Columbia, S.C., 1922.

Grosvenor, Verta [Verta Mae]. *Vibration Cooking or the Travel Notes of a Geechee Girl.* New York: Doubleday and Co., 1970.

Heyward, Dubose. "The Negro in the Low Country." *In The Carolina Low Country.* New York: Macmillan, 1931.

Hurston, Zora Neale. "Hoodoo in America." *Journal of American Folklore* 44 (October-December 1931): 317-417.

Hyatt, Harry Middleton. *Hoodoo-Conjuration-Witchcraft-Rootwork.* Vol. 3. St. Louis: Western Publishing Co., 1973.

Jackson, Juanita; Slaughter, Sabra; and Blake, J. "The Sea Islands as a Cultural Resource." *Black Scholar* 5 (March 1974): 32-39.

Jones-Jackson, Patricia. *When Roots Die; Endangered Traditions on the Sea Islands.* Athens: University of Georgia Press, 1987.

Josephy, Alvin M., Jr. *500 Nations; An Illustrated History of North American Indians.* New York: Alfred A. Knopf, 1994.

Joyner, Charles. *Down by the Riverside; A South Carolina Slave Community.* Urbana: University of Illinois Press, 1984.

Kemble, Frances Anne. *Journal of a Residence on A Georgian Plantation in 1838-1839.* New York: Harper and Brothers, Publishers, 1863.

Killion, Dr. Ronald G., and Walker, Dr. Charles T. *A Treasury of Georgia Folklore.* Atlanta: Cherokee Publishing Co., 1972.

Littlefield, Daniel C. *Rice and Slaves; Ethnicity and the Slave Trade in Colonial South Carolina.* Urbana and Chicago: University of Illinois Press, 1991.

Lloyd, John U. *History of the Vegetable Drugs of the Pharmacopeia of the United States.* Cincinnati: J. V. and C. G. Lloyd, 1911.

Meyer, Clarence. *American Folk Medicine.* New York: Thomas Y. Crowell Co., 1973.

Meyer, Joseph E. *The Herbalist.* Hammond, Ind.: Hammond Book Co., 1934.

Millspaugh, Dr. Charles F. *American Medicinal Plants: An Illustrative and Descriptive Guide to the American Plants Used as Homeopathic Remedies.* New York and Philadelphia: Boeriche and Tafel, 1887.

Moore, Colin, and Washington, Robert. *The Island Colonies: A Profile of Rural Poverty.* A report prepared for the United Methodist Church, August 1970.

Parsons, Elsie Clews. "Folklore of the Sea Islands, South Carolina." *Memoirs of the American Folklore Society* 16 (1923): 1-216.

Porcher, Francis P. "Report on the Indigenous Medical Plants of South Carolina." *Transactions of the American Medical Association* 2 (1849): 677-862.

Postell, William Dosite. *The Health of Slaves on Southern Plantations.* Baton Rouge: Louisiana State University Press, 1951.

Puckett, Dr. Newbell Niles. *Folk Beliefs of the Southern Negro.* Montclair, N.J.: Patterson Smith, 1968.

Rafinesque, C. S. *Medical Flora: or, Manual of the Medical Botany of the U.S. of North America.* 2 vols. Philadelphia: Atkinson and Alexander, 1828-1830.

Rogers, Dr. David. *The American Physician, Being a New System of Practice Founded on Botany.* Rochester, N.Y.: printed for the author by H. Leavenworth, 1824.

Savitt, Todd L. *Medicine and Slavery; The Diseases and Health Care of Blacks in Antebellum Virginia.* Urbana: University of Illinois Press, 1978.

Saxon, Lyle; Dreyer, Edward; Tallant, Robert. *Gumbo Ya-Ya.* Louisiana Writer's Project 1945. New York: Johnson Reprint Corp., 1969.

Smith, Peter, of the Miami Country. *The Indian Doctor's Dispensatory, Being Fa ther Smith's Advice Respecting Diseases and Their Cure.* Cincinnati: Brown and Looker, 1812. Reprinted in *Bulletin of the Lloyd Library of Botany, Pharmacy and Materia Medica.* Reproduction Series 2, Bulletin 2. 1901.

Snow, Loudell F. "Folk Medical Beliefs and Their Implications for Care of Patients: A Review Based on Studies Among Black Americans." *Annals of Internal Medicine* 81 (1974): 82-96.

Sperry, Dr. L. *The Botanic Family Physician: or, The Secret of Curing Diseases.* Cornwall, Vt.: published by the author, 1843.

Stampp, Kenneth M. *The Peculiar Institution: Slavery in the Ante-Bellum South.* New York: Vintage Books, 1956.

Turner, Lorenzo Dow. *Africanisms in the Gullah Dialect.* Ann Arbor: University of Michigan Press, 1974.

Vogel, Virgil J. *American Indian Medicine.* Norman: University of

Oklahoma Press, 1970.

Waring, Dr. Joseph Ioor. *A History of Medicine in South Carolina, 1670-1825.* 2 vols. Charleston: South Carolina Medical Association, 1964-67.

Weiner, Michael A. *Earth Medicine-Earth Foods: Plant Remedies, Drugs, and Natural Foods of the North American Indians.* New York: Macmillan, 1972.

Work, M. H. "Some Geechee Folk-Lore." *Southern Workman* 34 (November 1905): 633-35.

——————— "Some Geechee Folk-Lore Concluded." *Southern Workman* 34 (December 1905): 696-97.

Whitten, Norman E., Jr. "Contemporary Patterns of Malign Occultism Among Negroes in North Carolina." *Journal of American Folklore* 75 (October-December 1962): 311-25.

Wood, Peter H. *Black Majority; Negroes in Colonial South Carolina from 1670 through the Stono Rebellion.* New York: W.W. Norton and Company, 1975.

Woofter, T.J. Jr. *Black Yeomanry; Life on St. Helena Island.* New York: Henry Holt and Company, 1930.

## For Plants

Grimm, William Cary. *How to Recognize the Trees.* New York. Castle Books, 1962.

——————— *How to Recognize the Shrubs.* New York: Castle Books, 1966.

——————— *How to Recognize the Flowering Wild Plants.* New York: Castle Books, 1968.

Peterson, Roger Tory. *A Field Guide to Wildflowers.* Boston: Houghton Mifflin, 1968.

**Faith Mitchell** is a medical anthropologist whose original research includes African American communities in the U.S. and Caribbean. In her professional career she has focused on health and social policy in a variety of settings, including academia, the federal government, and philanthropy. Faith and her family live in Great Falls, Virginia.

Printed in Great Britain
by Amazon